APQ LIBRARY OF
PHILOSOPHY

APQ LIBRARY OF PHILOSOPHY
Nicholas Rescher, Editor

PLATO
ON BEAUTY, WISDOM, AND THE ARTS

EDITED BY

Julius Moravcsik

AND

Philip Temko

ROWMAN AND LITTLEFIELD
Totowa, New Jersey

First published in the United States 1982 by Rowman and Littlefield, 81 Adams Drive, Totowa, New Jersey 07512.

Distributed in the U.K. and Commonwealth by
George Prior Associated Publishers Limited
High Holborn House
53154 High Holborn
London WC1 V 6RL
England

Library of Congress Cataloging in Publication Data
Main entry under title:

Plato on beauty, wisdom, and the arts.

(APQ library of philosophy)
Bibliography: p.
Includes index.
Contents: Introduction / Julius Moravcsik,
Philip Temko — Plato on the triviality of
literature / Julia Annas — Noetic aspiration and
artistic inspiration / Julius Moravcsik — [etc.]
 1. Plato—Aesthetics—Congresses. 2. Aesthetics
—History—Congresses. I. Moravcsik, J. M. E.
II. Temko, Philip, 1924-   III. Series.
B398.A4P55   111.85   81-23434
ISBN 0-8476-7030-9   AACR2

Printed in the United States of America

Contents

v

Preface

These essays originated from the interdisciplinary conference on Plato's theories of art and beauty held at Bodega, California, on April 6 and 7, 1979—a workshop that brought together classicists, historians of philosophy, and aestheticians. The six main papers were presented by Julia Annas, Julius Moravcsik, Alexander Nehamas, Martha Craven Nussbaum, James O. Urmson, and Paul Woodruff.

The Bodega Conference was cosponsored by the National Endowment for the Humanities and the Sonoma State University Department of Philosophy. We are very grateful for the help we received from both these sponsors.

The impetus for organizing the conference (and this volume) came from some remarks made five years ago in Detroit by a fine young American poet, Patricia Hooper Everhardus. Ms. Everhardus wanted to know how Plato, the philosopher who used poetic images more than anyone else, could talk about art the way he did. It was embarrassing not to have been able to provide her with enough recent material dealing with this question, but it meant discovering that not enough is available. We hope this volume will contribute toward answering this and related questions, which, we are sure, reverberate in the minds of many thoughtful readers of Plato.

Introduction

The contemporary problem of the relationship between science and the humanities mirrors a key problem in Plato's philosophy— that is, the relationship between his insistence on purely rational and logical approaches to reality, and his own conscious use of poetic and other literary forms in the dialogues, as well as his explicit acknowledgment of the importance of appreciating beauty. How did Plato resolve the tension between the appreciation of beauty and artistic forms of expression on the one hand, and an approach to reality that held up a science like mathematics as the paradigm? Or did Plato see the whole problem in a different light? Perhaps there are some important differences between his basic categories and those employed in contemporary philosophic and scientific thought. If this is so, then the unearthing of such differences could greatly enrich both our historical understanding and our view of our own situation by providing us with a strikingly different way of looking at the cognitive role of the arts and the supposed antagonism between science and the humanities.

Ironically, Plato has been both the inspiration of many poets and musicians, and also the object of wrath of many humanists who are shocked by what they take to be his condemnation of the "fine arts." It is time to take a hard look at the nature of this "condemnation."

Here, then, are some of the major problems that the papers of this volume wrestle with: How can Plato condemn poetry when his own writings abound with metaphor and simile, not to mention his frequent and striking use of myth? On what grounds is Plato insisting that art and its products must be assessed from a moral point of view? Why is one of his main themes the issue of whether art is good for us? What criteria does one use to answer such a question? We know that the Greeks did not have a word that corresponds exactly to the modern English expression "art." Thus we must examine carefully what it is that is condemned in the *Republic*. Is it all that we would call "fine arts" today? Or only poetry and drama? Or only certain types of poetry and drama? Further, there is the problem of the extent to which art can provide knowledge and understanding. Plato insists that this is an important question and seems to answer it quite negatively. Evidently his view is that art provides no insight or understanding. What are we to make of the various statements that seem to express such a strong position? Finally, there is the issue of internal consistency, and the possibility of development in Plato's thought. Are the books of the *Republic* consistent with each other on the topic of art? Does the *Phaedrus* present a different view from that presented in the *Republic?* What is the impact of the psychological theory of the *Phaedrus* on the view of beauty and art presented in that dialogue?

These essays will not solve all the problems of interpreting Plato on art and beauty. But they solve some problems, shed light on others, bring still others into new perspective, and attest to the lasting significance of Plato's philosophizing on these topics.

JULIUS MORAVCSIK
PHILIP TEMKO

Plato on the Triviality of Literature

Julia Annas

"Literature" may, of course, be a misleading word to use in connection with Plato; it tends to suggest to us the private reading of books, mainly novels or biographies, whereas Plato's main concern is with the public recitation of dramatic or epic poetry. Right from the start there are at least two large differences between our concern with literature and Plato's concern with poetry. One is that for him music belongs with poetry and is not a separate art (indeed, he finds purely instrumental music disturbing and degenerate[1]), whereas for us opera, for example, is typically thought of as a mixed genre. The other is that at least in the *Republic* Plato is uninterested in prose, at any rate the role of written prose.[2] There he ignores the status of works of history like those of Herodotus and Thucydides[3]; there is no sign of either the *Gorgias*' hostility to or the *Phaedrus*' rehabilitation of prose oratory; and he shows no serious concern with written works of prose fiction.[4] The *Republic*'s "ancient quarrel" is between philosophy and *poetry*.[5] Nevertheless, in spite of these striking differences I shall talk of Plato's attitude to literature and not just to poetry, both because what he says about poetry would clearly apply to all literature in a modern context, and because it is still rewarding to focus on Plato's attitude to artistic products of a literary nature as opposed to the fine arts and the visual arts.

I shall begin from a striking fact about the treatment of the poets in the *Republic*. In books 2 and 3 Plato pays a great deal of attention to literature. He begins by attacking the poets for saying dangerously false things about the gods; this is the initial reason for censoring Homer and other poets. But Plato then goes far beyond his original reason for dealing with the poets. The literature surrounding us, we are told, influences our characters in every way, and so poets must be censored and directed not only in what they say about the gods, but also in their works as a whole. Their influence on people is not limited to a few matters but is all-pervasive, extending even to styles and manners. Plato launches on a long discussion of the form of poetry as well as its subjects, putting forward his own ideas about the dangers of the kind of poetry that has the reciter imitate or represent a character, rather than merely narrating what happened. Finally a long and eloquent passage (400e–402d) tells us the crucial importance of what might have looked like a digression. Not just poetry, we are told, but also all the arts are vital for their effect in creating and sustaining kinds of character. The right kind of art helps to produce people with an unflawed love of what is good and attractive, while bad art and literature produce a conflicted and degraded character. All this fits well with Plato's great stress, in the *Republic*, on virtue as being a matter of character; the stress on education to produce a person of a distinctive type prepares us for the account of justice as a state of the soul rather than the fulfillment of a set of duties. The arts have a crucial role to play because they affect the development of the young, who must form the right habits. And literature is the most important—at any rate, it is the art Plato begins from and in terms of which his whole discussion is carried on, the other arts being introduced only briefly before the general conclusion.[6] In book 3, then, we are made aware, vividly and at length, of the great *importance* of literature.

In book 10, on the other hand, Plato seems to be concerned to stress how *un*important literature is. The poet's works are at "third remove from the truth"; he lacks both knowledge and true belief about his subject matter; nobody who could make both a thing and a copy of it would bother with the latter or take it seriously.[7] "I think that, if he truly had knowledge of the things he imitates, he would much rather devote himself to actions than to the imitation of them, and that he would try to leave behind many fine actions as memorials of himself and be eager to be the subject of a eulogy rather than the author of it."[8] Plato even claims that people really despise poets and reserve their honors and respect for people who achieve practical aims.

Why does Plato move from treating literature as important to treating it as trivial?

One obvious answer is that he thinks that it is trivial *in itself* and important only for its educative value. In book 3 he is concerned with forming young minds; by the time we get to book 10 we have seen the life of the mature Guardians and their search for truth and the good, and art and literature seem poor things by comparison.[9]

Now certainly there is no contradiction in thinking literature immensely important in education but despising a life devoted to it. All the same, I am not convinced that this point exhausts the interest of Plato's shift of attitude between these two books of the *Republic*. There are real difficulties in the way of a single coherent account doing justice to both books, and stressing them may illuminate the apparent change in Plato's attitude to literature, and its relation to the other arts.

In book 3, as already mentioned, the paradigmatic art form is poetry. Plato does not mention the other arts at all until, at 401ff, he simply asserts that painting, weaving, architecture and the applied arts all have the important feature that has been explained at length in the case of literature, namely affecting the character and producing either a harmonious, integrated person (400d11ff) or the reverse. It is because of this, Plato says, that not just poets but also the other craftsmen must make only graceful and beautiful products (401b). Now one important consequence of poetry's being the model art form is that the important notion of imitation or mimesis is introduced solely in terms of poetry. At 392dff the difference between mimesis and narration is introduced ostensively by a passage of the *Iliad* where a transition is made from narration to direct speech; a great deal is made of this point, and there is a long discussion of the extent and type of poetry thus mimetic that is to be allowed. The control and direction of poetry as an educative force is developed in a way that requires a sharp distinction between the mimetic and nonmimetic kinds. We are then told abruptly that the other art forms are equally important in forming character, and that they too must be controlled and make none but correct products. But if we ask how this distinction between mimetic and nonmimetic is to be carried over to the other arts, we are left baffled. What could correspond to the distinction between narration and direct speech in the case of painting? weaving? worst of all, architecture?[10] Plato does not raise these questions, because he treats the other arts so casually. We are left holding that there *is* a distinction between beneficial and harmful pictures, rugs, and buildings, but with no idea of what it is that makes the difference.

What Plato says about mimesis in book 3 has been criticized for its "simpleminded" psychology, namely the idea that we become like people that we imitate or represent. I am not concerned with that point here, though actually I think that it is not at all simpleminded to hold that we become like the people whose actions we imitate, and that the point was well taken by Aristotle.[11] What interests me here is simply the point that literature, and poetry in particular, is paramount as an example of the importance and influence of the arts, to the extent that the criterion for being good or harmful art is put in terms of mimesis that have no clear application to any art but poetry.

In book 10 the position is reversed: the paradigm art form is painting, and mimesis is introduced in terms appropriate to painting. This is of the greatest importance for the trivializing of poetry and literature in book 10. To bring this out I shall look at the two famous arguments designed to show that art in general is worthless.

The first argument claims to show that artists lack knowledge (595a–602c). We are struck from the first by the fact that although Plato had introduced the topic of imitative *poetry*, as though this were all that would concern him, he at once goes on to tell us what imitation is in terms of *painting*.[12] The craftsman who copies the Form and produces a bed is compared with the painter who copies the way the bed appears; mimesis here is the literal copying of one visual aspect of a thing, the way it looks (598a), and is explicitly compared to holding up a mirror to reflect things (596d–e). Obviously this performance requires no knowledge, nor even the craftsman's true belief.

Why does Plato make painting the paradigm art form here? Those who have noticed this have not been sufficiently worried by it.[13] It is not enough to assert that Plato naturally thought in visual terms, that "Plato's preoccupation with images—the visual slant of his imagination—is so pronounced as to amount almost to an obsession."[14] Book 3 does not give us that impression; and I doubt that Plato's imagination had a visual slant anyway. Surely no one with a visual imagination would have written as he does of dialectic pulling the soul's eye out of the mud.[15] Many of Plato's images stay in the mind precisely because they are so bizarre and visually incoherent.[16] A more interesting puzzle is why Plato concentrates on not just painting, but also the limited case of painting that aims at "photographic realism" and *trompe-l 'oeil* effects, representing the painter as trying to deceive people, if only children and fools and at a distance, into thinking that the painted cobbler is a real one. Elsewhere in the *Republic* painting has a more expansive and honorable role.[17] Of course, painting of the kind he considers does exist;[18] the question is why he thinks that this has anything to do with poetry. In due course I hope we shall see a plausible answer to this.

The account of painting that made the painter into a mindless copier of appearances is carried over to poetry (598d7) and applied to Homer and the tragedians. The point to be taken over is that the artist, in whatever medium, produces without *knowledge* of his product. This was already said to be true of the tragic poet, in the middle of the argument about painting (597e6–8): He too is an imitator who produces something "at three removes from nature" requiring no comprehension of what is imitated.

But does the claim about the artist's lack of knowledge carry over from painting to poetry? It does not, because of the very narrow way the painter's activity has been described. Homer cannot be said to copy the appearances of things in anything like the way that the illusionistic painter does. What corresponds to holding up the mirror, or capturing the perspective of the way a bed looks from one particular angle of vision? There seems no analogy at all.

It may be objected that it is inept to expect every detail of the visual case to carry over; what matters is that the poet's product is, like the painter's, at third remove from real nature. But we cannot just use expressions like "third from the truth" of the poet's work, as Plato does, as though it were obvious what they meant when applied to poetry. In the context, the only obvious way we have of understanding them is by reference to the metaphysical picture of Form, particular, and copy on which the descriptions of the painter depended. Yet it is hardly obvious that the picture has any application to poetry. And Plato discusses the poet's lack of knowledge, at 601c–602b, in terms strikingly in conflict with that picture. Now we are told that knowledge is possessed by the *user* of a thing, true belief by the maker, and neither by the imitator. If we ask where in this picture the Form fits, an answer is hard to come by; Forms are not used, and the contrast is no longer between Forms and particulars, but between using and making the same particular object, a bridle or a flute. Plato is here discussing the difference between knowledge and belief, and the poet's deficiencies, in everyday terms (which are well taken, for we can readily grasp that the user has knowledge that the producer may lack) that have no reference to Forms. It would have been perfectly easy for Plato to have drawn the distinction in terms of Forms and particular instances. He could have said that the poet has no knowledge of the Forms of justice, courage, and so on, but merely copies particular instances of actions that are just or courageous, thus failing to show us moral reality, because any such action will inevitably be qualified and imperfect by reason of its individual circumstances. Such an argument would be attractive, not least because it would need only the moral Forms familiar from the central books, without the problematic Form of Bed. In fact, Plato insists on the Form of Bed for the description of the painter, and strikingly fails to appeal to the more familiar Forms. The argument here makes no reference to them; most of the points are familiar already from the *Apology* and *Ion*.[19] The poet gives a plausible description of generals, but in fact knows nothing about generals and what they are and do; he could not be one, or give any kind of reasoned account of a general's decision; and so forth. Whatever the merits of this line of thought, it does not entitle Plato to talk of the poet's work in terms like "third from the truth"; for these terms have been given sense only within the model of Form, particular, and copy used to describe the painter's work. And that model does not fit the poet's lack of knowledge, nor the way Plato characterizes that lack.[20]

So the reasons for saying that the painter lacks knowledge do not carry over to the poet; and Plato, in fact, gives a separate argument to show that the poet is ignorant of his subject matter. But then Plato has done nothing to show us that it is legitimate to talk of the poet in terms appropriate to the painter, as being "third from the truth" or as "imitating" in a way that merely mirrors. Nothing has been said to show us that the poet "imitates" *in the way that the painter does*. But in book 10 no other sense has been suggested. And we cannot appeal to book 3 to fill out the sense in which the poet "imitates", for in book 3 mimesis is not what Homer does, but what the person reciting Homer does, when he comes to the bits of Homer that are in direct speech. In book 3 the distinction between mimetic and nonmimetic poetry applied *within* poetry, so it cannot elucidate what goes on in book 10 when poetry as a whole is said to imitate. This difficulty about the shift in range of 'mimesis' has been noted often enough. One result of it is that in book 10 we have *no* idea of what it is for the poet to imitate, other than that which is given by the comparison with the painter. But, as we have seen, precisely this is the disputable point: Why should the painter provide a good comparison?

The second attempt to show that all art is worthless goes from 602c–605c. Scene painting relies upon optical illusions of various kinds: flat surfaces seem three-dimensional, just as straight sticks look bent in water, and concave surfaces can be made to appear convex. In such cases, part of the soul is taken in and accepts the appearance at face value, but the reasoning part relies on objective procedures of "measuring, counting, and weighing" and discovers the real state of affairs. Now this means that two parts of the soul are in conflict; clearly the reasoning part, which appeals to objective criteria, is the better part; so painting appeals to the inferior part of the soul, whose worthlessness is dwelled on. Then Plato asks if the same applies to poetry. He realizes that his argument does not carry straight over; for when Socrates asks if the same is true of poetry, which appeals to hearing, as is true of painting, which appeals to sight, Glaucon facilely agrees, but Socrates insists that the point be separately argued for poetry. Nonetheless, Plato clearly thinks that there is a parallel here. But again it is far from clear that there is. Poetry, he says, appeals to and strengthens the lower, desiring part of the soul, which resists reason. Poetry encourages short-term indulgence in our emotions when reason would forbid their gratification because it is useless or harmful for the agent if he considers his life as a whole. Reason appears here as the capacity enabling the agent to achieve moral distance and not be dominated by his emotions at any one time.

Now this argument, clearly, works only if the division of the soul is the same in each case–that is, if the opposition to reason set up by painting is the same as the one set up by poetry. But they are not the same,[21] for it is absurd to suggest that the strength of one's desires has anything to do with one's proneness to accept optical illusions at face value. Further, the lower part of the soul to which poetry appeals is, we are told, one that itself gives scope for imitaton; it is the tendency to be led by emotion that provides most of tragedy's best plots. But this can hardly be the same as the hasty or unreflective acceptance of visual impressions that leads one to think that a straight stick in water is actually bent. The latter can happen to anyone, and is not a particularly rich source of dramatic material. In the case of both painting and poetry, reason enters as the reflective and careful corrector of first impressions; but its role in protecting us from acting on wrong visual impressions is hardly the same as its role in protecting us from acting on the feelings of the moment by giving us a correct estimate of the moral importance of the past and the future.

Once again, it would have been quite possible, and more in consonance with the rest of the *Republic*, for Plato to have made his point about the part of the soul to which poetry appeals in a way that was more parallel to the argument about the painter. He could have carried over the contrast between appearance and reality, and presented the poet as one who presents us with judgments that concern merely moral appearance and not moral reality, as indicated by their fragmentary and often conflicting nature. (The poets' moral viewpoint would be no more advanced than that of many of Socrates' interlocutors in early Platonic dialogues, who hold isolated and latently contradictory moral opinions because they have never subjected their beliefs to rational tests for consistency.) Reason would appear as the source of deliberated and authoritative moral views that sort out, and may conflict with, our prereflective intuitions, which tend to be based on the mere appeal of particular people and actions.[22] Once again, Plato strikingly fails to carry through what could have been a plausible parallel; his actual argument against poetry rests on its ability to stir up a part of us that is irritable enough already and ought to be kept quiet, with no reference to any distinction between appearance and reality.

One escape from this difficulty lies in claiming that Plato does not even intend the parts of the soul to be the same in the two contrasts with reason. On this view Plato regards the part of the soul opposed to reason as a collection of undesirable tendencies rather than a unity. This is supported by his language in two passages, 603a7 and 605a8–b2. In the first of these he says that the part of the soul that opposes measure and calculation is "one of the worthless things in us"; and in the second he says that the poet is like the painter in appealing not to the best part of the soul but to some other part. Both these statements are consistent with the claim that the part of the soul concerned is different for poetry and painting; and both are worded vaguely enough to suggest that claim. But this defense gives away too much, for it deprives Plato of any argument. If the opposition to reason has a quite different source in the visual case from that in the literary case, then Plato has no semblance of justification for moving from the worthlessness of painting to that of poetry and abusing the latter in terms appropriate to the former.[23]

So in this argument also the case made against painting does not carry over to poetry; Plato has simply become confused here. No doubt his eagerness to reach the conclusion prevents him from the careful examination of his premises that would have revealed the confusion. Reason is always the hero of the soul, and the part that opposes reason is always described in uncomplimentary terms as the worthless or trashy part. Plato fails to see that what is trashy about the trashy part is different for painting and for poetry. A sign of this is that in this passage he always refers to it merely as the trashy part, keeping in the background the fact that it is the *desiring* part; in the context of this argument this would have made it all too clear that desire has nothing to do with optical illusions.

In both these arguments we find Plato making an unsuccessful attempt to apply to poetry considerations that apply only to painting. This is more than a local weakness in Plato's argumentative capacities, for it is bound up with the fact that poetry and literature, so important in book 3, are presented as trivial in book 10. For the charges that poetry is trivial and worthless are all based on the comparison with painting; and so they must fail to the extent that that does. We are told that the poet is despised because he devotes his life to making images instead of originals, which is a pointless exercise; he deals with images of virtue only; he is at third remove from the truth; he lacks knowledge and even true belief because he deals only in imáges; he is an imitator and as such is held in low regard; his imitation consorts with an inferior part of the soul and that is why he goes in for easy popularity, because most people lack the discernment to see his products for what they are, mindless products appealing to the mindless part of the soul.[24] Now, all these charges of triviality are given their sense by the analogy with painting, for, as we have seen, the way that terms like "imitation" were introduced in book 3 did not in themselves have implications of worthlessness. The famous phrases of contempt that have become so notorious, all spring from the attempt to "see" poetry in terms of painting.

This shows up vividly if we turn to the third argument (605c–608b). Surprisingly, Plato says that the gravest indictment of imitation has yet to be brought. "It is able to corrupt even good men, with very few exceptions, and . . . is a very dangerous thing" (605c8). Art and especially poetry encourages all the lower desires and makes them hard to cope with. The part of us that takes pleasure in seeing others' sufferings in the theater is the part that longs to indulge its own; taking pleasure in laughing at comedies tends to affect our attitudes in real life and to make us cynical and unserious. "So too with sex, anger, and all the desires, pleasures and pains that we say follow us in every activity. Poetic imitation fosters these in us. It nurtures and waters them when they ought to wither; it places them in command in our soul when they ought to obey in order that we might become better and happier men instead of worse and more miserable." (606d1–7). We must reject the guidance of Homer and the tragic poets, crass though it may seem, because "the struggle to be good or bad is important." (608b4–5)

At first glance this argument looks like nothing but a more rhetorical repetition of what was said in the second: Poetry fosters the lower part of the soul against the rule of the higher part, reason. But in fact they are quite different, and three major dissonances show up. First, Plato here takes poetry seriously in its own right; Homer is recognized as a major factor in many people's moral lives—some even saying that he is the educator of Greece. The banishment of poetry is recognized as needing an explanation because of its importance, which Plato does not here deny. In the first argument, however, Plato would have had us believe that people do not really regard Homer and his like as very significant, unlike the real moral teachers, like Pythagoras. Second, Plato has given up talking of poetry in visual terms; he talks straightforwardly about what goes on in the theater and its effect on people and their emotions, with no use of the notion of "images." And third, poetry comes in as a competitor to the truly moral way to live one's life; it is a temptation to stray from the path, one that can mislead and corrupt even good men. In the first two arguments, however, the triviality of poetry was presented as such that no good and intelligent person could plausibly be so much as tempted by it. In all these respects this third argument is like the discussion in book 3. Poetry is seen as *dangerous*: Homer can make one stray from the path of virtue, and so the pleasures of poetry, which are not denied, must be removed. The only difference is that in book 3 poetry was to be heavily censored and controlled, but not banished entirely, whereas in book 10 Plato is more pessimistic about the ability of even the good to resist its attractions, and Homer is banished.

I began by saying that Plato appears to treat poetry as important in book 3 and trivial in book 10; but we can now see that he also treats it as important in part of book 10, namely the third argument that follows the notorious two that assimilate poetry to painting. We have two attitudes, and the gap between them cannot be explained away by differences of purpose or interest in different parts of the *Republic*. Not only are there all the conflicts between books 3 and 10 that have so often been noticed (the scope of "mimesis," for example) and that have led people to argue that book 10 was originally a separate piece of writing, or added later.[25] In book 10 we can see Plato arguing rhetorically to the conclusion that poetry is a dangerous rival to morality, on the basis of arguments that try to show that poetry is so trivial that no sensible person would bother with it. The strangeness of this needs some explanation. We can see by now that a key role is played by the attempt to assimilate poetry to the status of painting. In book 3, and in the third argument of book 10, Plato treats poetry seriously and realistically; he takes people's estimate of the poets at face value and argues that this influence produces genuine pleasure but is morally dangerous. He wavers on how to deal with the subversive force of poetry, and book 10 is more severe than book 3. But both these passages conflict with the first two arguments in book 10, where Plato argues, unsuccessfully and with great strain, that poetry is like painting, flies in the face of most people's estimate of the significance of poetry, and claims on the basis of the analogy that he has set up that poetry is too trivial to bother with, a poor, pathetic thing like scene painting.

So, rather than say that Plato thought that poetry was trivial, and important only for its educative effects, I would prefer to say that he always thought that poetry was extremely important and dangerous in its own right, and that he had a split attitude to it. Sometimes he thinks that the influence of poetry must be accepted as a fact and coped with in moral education (he wavers over how to do this, at times, as in book 3, trying to tame the classics of poetry and at times, as in the third argument of book 10, discarding them totally). But sometimes he feels that he must prove that poetry really is trivial and obviously facile, and so not even a factor in moral education or the good life. There does seem to me to be a lasting conflict, one not easily resolved, between accepting that poetry is important and dangerous, and trying to *prove* that it is trivial. The conflict shows up particularly sharply in book 10, where Plato argues that poetry is really trivial, and then pleads earnestly for the need to reject it as being tempting but dangerous. For surely the argument must be either too weak or too strong; if the first two arguments are successful, then poetry is so obviously worthless that there is no need of any further argument to show why it should be discarded, and no question of good, morally serious people being tempted by it. Whereas if there *is* need of a further argument, and good men *can* really be seduced, then the arguments to show that poetry is superficial and worthless cannot be good arguments. They must have missed the mark.

There has been a constant tendency to argue that Plato's attitude to art and poetry is not really split, and that different passages can be reconciled. I do not think that this can be done; but I agree that it is not enough just to notice difficulties and disagreements in what Plato says. There ought to be some explanation of how Plato is led to say inconsistent things, some account of the reasons leading him either way; otherwise one would be justified in suspecting that the contradictions were merely superficial ones, created by differences in expressing basically the same point of view. I shall try to support the conclusion I have reached by analyzing the arguments of book 10, and do so by showing that the split is not local to book 10; it goes deep in Plato's thought. Because of the dangers of being overly general here, and also because it makes my point most clearly, I shall do this indirectly. I shall compare Plato's attitude to the arts in general with that of two other thinkers who are like him in several important respects. They recognize in art a powerful force for good or evil in the training and maintenance of character; they are highly revisionary in their claims about the worth of what is commonly taken to be good art; they are moral reformers of society, intent upon bringing about a world where people's social relations will be improved and transformed; and they are people sensitive to art who feel the need to judge art harshly. I hope that this comparison will show why it is tempting to ascribe to Plato a single coherent view about art. It assimilates him to a modern view (of which I offer two representatives) that we find easily comprehensible and appropriate for someone with the kind of moral theory that Plato holds. This viewpoint is, very roughly, that art is to be judged as good or bad, acceptable or not, by its social value. My examples will try to bring out how this viewpoint can be essentially the same even given the most diverse opinions on what the right values are that are to be attained. In modern versions we find much that suggests book 3 and the third argument of book 10; and it is no accident that Plato's views on art are often thought to be of this kind. But this viewpoint excludes the kind of total trivializing of the arts that Plato attempts, in the case of poetry, in the first two arguments of book 10. So the modern parallels stress by contrast the importance of these arguments in showing us the divide in Plato's mind. The notorious two arguments show us that Plato's view is ineliminably different from modern views to which it seems most akin. I shall end by offering some suggestions as to why this should be so.

An obvious parallel to Plato's moralistic onslaught on art is Tolstoy's *What Is Art?*[26] Tolstoy attacks most contemporary art for being depraved and elitist, so corrupt as to be not really art at all but what he calls "counterfeit." He recognizes the implausibility of an account of art that results in the rejection of most of what people have been brought up to think of as examples of great art, but insists that this is irrelevant to the truth. Most "art," he claims, is bad and counterfeit because it aims only at pleasure; art is something quite different. When we clear away all the vague and rubbishy definitions and academic irrelevancies, we can see that art is the way in which one person successfully gets across to another some sincere feeling, and so good art will be art that transmits worthwhile feelings, and bad art, art that transmits worthless feelings or fails to transmit anything at all. Good art is morally serious, not frivolous. In Tolstoy this idea is bound up with his belief that good feelings are feelings of universal brotherhood, accessible to all. When the world is morally better, "there will be one common, brotherly universal art; and then first, that art will naturally be rejected that transmits feelings incompatible with the religious perception of our time—feelings that do not unite, but divide men—and later, that insignificant, exclusive art to which an unmerited importance is now attributed will be rejected."[27] Plato's concern with fraternity is more authoritarian, but we can see the same underlying idea: Good art promotes the right ideas, and bad art is bad because it prevents people from developing them.

What Is Art? contains many famous passages that bring out forcefully the triviality and real banality lying behind sentimental and pretentious attitudes to art (especially highly stylized arts like opera). But it would be clearly wrong to conclude that Tolstoy thought that art itself was trivial. What angers him about the triviality of what passes for art is precisely that it throws people off and blinds them to the existence and significance of real art. Real art, for Tolstoy, is very important in the good life; and this point stands independently of his eccentric views on what constitutes real art, and the aesthetic superiority of simple and uneducated taste.

My other example is Tolstoy's contemporary, the critic Cherny-shevsky,[28] who although little known in his own right in the West is historically important as being the effective source of the doctrine of socialist realism. His influence cannot be held responsible for the low quality of work actually achieved by those producing art and literature in those countries where socialist realism is the dominant theory of art,[29] but the theory is of interest apart from that, and it is intriguing that the ideology of art in, for example, Soviet Russia owes its form much less to Marxist ideas than to writers like Chernyshevsky, who stand in the tradition of utilitarianism, making the general good part of the social purpose of art.[30] (Mill, interestingly, has a most unutilitarian approach to art and literature, and the aesthetics of utilitarianism are much better represented in the nineteenth-century Russian critics, who were influenced by Mill's political and economic ideas, but not by his aesthetics.[31] No doubt this owes something to the influential position of writers in Russian society, making their works more obvious sources of general utility than they are in the calculations of Western utilitarians, by whom creative writing has usually been perceived as relaxation and entertainment, rather than as a dynamic source of social change.)

Chernyshevsky is like Tolstoy in having a very revisionary moral theory; it is indeed a morality for revolutionaries. In its light Chernyshevsky rejects much of contemporary art and literature as pandering only to idle pleasures; the life devoted to art is denounced as being morally worthless. This is because he denies that art has an independent worth that gives life meaning. It is the other way around; art derives its meaning and significance from life. Like Tolstoy, Chernyshevsky rejects inflated Hegelian claims that art has transcendent value because it strives valiantly to embody the perfect Idea in a particular form that must necessarily fall short. "The essential purpose of art is to reproduce everything in life that is of interest to man."[32] Although he takes some pains to insist that by "reproducing" he does not mean mindless copying or "daguerreotype realism,"[33] Chernyshevsky stresses that art is not something with independent value; the only point of art (and literature can do this best) is so to describe and reproduce reality as to explain it in a way encouraging the good, progressive elements in life, and bringing about improvement of character in the reader. Art is only "a substitute for reality in the case of its absence," poetry is only a reference book to prepare one for reality and jog one's memory on details. This insistence that art does nothing more than reproduce reality and that its value derives from its effectiveness and utility in so doing, does not spring from philistinism;[34] Chernyshevsky was a literary critic who could show great receptiveness and sensitivity, and his view of art and literature derives rather from his sense of the urgency of taking a moral viewpoint on it.[35]

Here too we would be wrong to infer from the numerous attempts to deflate aesthetic pretensions that Chernyshevsky thinks that art itself is trivial. Manifestly he does not; it has enormous importance in getting people to accept progressive ideas (his own novel *What Is to Be Done?* was intended to be thus influential, and was). The undermining of pretentious claims for art is necessary to pave the way for art's true role and importance. Thus we must not assume that Chernyshevsky intended to show that art was trivial because of some of his more downright pronouncements, like the notorious "it must be admitted that our art has been unable to create anything like an orange or an apple, let alone the luxurious fruit of tropical lands,"[36] or the comment that seascapes are useful because they show people living in the middle of the Russian plains what the sea looks like. These statements taken in isolation look very like the scornful attitude of the first two arguments of book 10 of the *Republic;* but in fact Chernyshevsky is insistent that art does not reproduce reality in a trivial way, and indeed takes some pains to claim that this is not what Plato meant by mimesis either. (Like many another, he interprets book 10 in the light of book 3 with scant regard for consistency.) His fundamental position is that art is very important because it can affect people for the better or for the worse; art is only trivial when it does not even attempt to do this but merely indulges the writer's own concerns without care for the welfare of others. In practice Chernyshevsky rates writers as good or bad according to whether they do or do not reflect and further the current of progressive ideas (though he is far from crude in his interpretation of this).

Tolstoy and Chernyshevsky share with Plato some broad but

clear similarities of outlook. They differ very widely over what they take to be the right moral end: Tolstoy finds it in Christian brotherhood, and Chernyshevsky, in the rationally organized communal society. But they agree in finding that the viewpoint of morality imposes the necessity of taking a moral view of art and literature. Art cannot just be accepted at its own valuation; the claims of its practitioners must be scrutinized from a moral point of view, and it is morality that provides the standard of art. The "aesthetic" view, that art has its own end, with intrinsic standards that cannot be subordinated to aims of another kind, is harshly rejected—and with it much of what calls itself art. In the rhetoric with which they refuse the claims of contemporary artists and writers to be doing something of significance just by producing a work of art, both Tolstoy and Chernyshevsky often recall Plato's fierce moralism in books 2 and 3 of the *Republic;* they also, in different ways, show the same kind of regret, the same feeling of strain produced in a sensitive and artistic person by the perceived necessity to overturn the claims of art as they have been put forward and understood. (Plato is said to have burned the tragedies he had written, after hearing Socrates; Tolstoy came to consign all his own works to the category of bad art, except the two stories *The Prisoner of the Caucasus* and *God Sees the Truth but Waits.*)

Now in book 3, and in the third argument of book 10, Plato's position seems to be recognizably like this. Morality gives us an independent standard that judges between good and bad art; the censoring of Homer and the tragedians is just the application of this standard. But bad art is still art, as recognized by poets and listeners; Plato is not denying that the poets are really creating genuine works of art, but rather accepting this and arguing that this is not a sufficient ground for allowing them to propagate morally harmful ideas. Further, and importantly, book 3 leaves open the possibility of *good* poetry; like Tolstoy and Chernyshevsky, Plato envisages a literature of the future that will create and sustain good people. Admittedly, he is vague here, and wavers. The good man's style, though confusingly called "unmixed," is allowed to retain *some* imitation,[37] and the censoring of Homer will presumably leave *something*; so apparently there will be some recognizable but approved poetry. Plato's vagueness here is understandable, for if you think that most present art is morally corrupt then you may well distrust your intuitions as to what sort of art is morally pure. (Tolstoy fortunately makes this qualification to his own choice of samples of good art.) In book 10 we can see Plato giving up and rejecting all generally recognized art as being hopelessly corrupt, though even then he relents a little at the last moment and lets in "hymns to the gods and eulogies of good men" (607a), which will formally resemble some of what has been rejected. But we can understand even the waverings here as just uncertainty about the moral potential of art and literature; both in book 3 and in the final argument of book 10 there is no wavering on the point that it is morality that determines what (if any) is good art.

But the two arguments of book 10 that trivialize art give us a different picture. For the arguments that try to reduce poetry to the level of *trompe-l'oeil* painting erase the significance of the moral distinction between good and bad poetry: *all* poetry is now seen as so trivial and silly that it falls right beneath the scope of moral concern. To indulge in it at all is to display weakness of character and superficiality; it appeals both in producer and consumer to the lowest part of the soul, the part that should be ruled by reason and not allowed autonomous development. It is not a thing that could have any real value, any more than the efforts of the chef and the delight of the gourmet. Plato talks here as though all poetry, including Homer, were utterly stupid. It is as if he were regarding them all as something like the products of a mass culture like TV shows, something so essentially banal that it is hard to see what could be distinctively worth having about a good specimen. The problem of the relation of poetry and morality, the possible bad effects of Homer and the tragedians, that so exercised Plato in book 3, has been drastically "solved" by the arguments that recast the problem; poetry does not have the standing even to enter into moral consideration, for it is as marginal as scene painting and optical illusions.

Both the fierce moralist like Tolstoy, and the utilitarian socialist realist, think of art as important, and of literature as especially important, because of its role in moral education and in creating the emotionally sustaining background of the good life. It is in terms of a moral criterion that they draw the line between good and bad art and insist on rejecting what is perceived as worthless according to it. Book 3 and the last argument of book 10 might well indicate that Plato held a similar view; the difference between these passages lies in increased pessimism about the scope for poetry in the good life, not in a fundamental change of attitude. But the two intrusive arguments in book 10 prevent us from taking Plato to endorse this attitude wholeheartedly. The desperate attempt to prove poetry trivial by assimilating it to another art form is meant to remove poetry from the range of morality because of its very nature, not because of its morally bad effects. Poetry here is too pathetic even to be wicked.

There has always been the strongest temptation, from Plotinus onward, to give Plato a single coherent theory of art, by claiming that in the book 10 arguments he is attacking only blankly realist art as being bad (perhaps with contemporary developments in view) and that book 3 shows that he leaves a place for the true and inspired artist who will not just copy slices of life but also will "imitate" and represent ideals, the Forms of various virtues and morally desirable states. Thus the superficial poet, who copies banalities and aims only at pleasure, can be banished, while room can be left for the profound poet to help and prepare the ground for the philosopher's work.[38] There are grave *prima facie* objections to this idea; it is strained to assume that when we read of the banishment of all poetry in book 10 we are to think that all the same a place *has* been left for good poetry. But all the same, the temptation is very natural. We would like Plato not to be a philistine about poetry. We would like the *Republic* to be a coherent whole. We would like to account for the passage at 402a–c where "forms" of some kind are embodied in art and poetry, and the passages where the philosopher and statesman is compared to a poet or a painter.[39] And, as should be clear by now, there is also a deeper temptation. We wish to assimilate Plato's attitude to one that we find easily comprehensible, and, above all, appropriate to the committed moral reformer. We are familiar with the attitude that we find in Tolstoy and Chernyshevsky, and we can see that they have basically the same approach to art and literature in spite of the vast difference of their moral views. They see art as having no independent claim to significance; good art is not good because it meets some standard internal to the aesthetic enterprise, but because it contributes to a morally worthy end, whether that end be the spread of Christian brotherly feelings, the coming of the revolution, or the realization of the ideal state. This attitude has become familiar, and we take it for granted as a coherent and tenable position in aesthetic controversies even if we think that it is wrong.

I have suggested that Plato does not consistently adopt this familiar position. In book 3 we can see him drawn to the idea of reforming poetry in the service of a morally worthy end; elsewhere we find him treating it as below serious moral consideration. He is deeply split about art, and especially about poetry. In the *Republic* he treats poetry, inconsistently, as both trivial and dangerous because he is pulled both ways; he wants to tame poetry in the service of morality and to expel it from morality's concern altogether. Attempts to reconcile books 3 and 10 on the basis of examining selected passages or scrutinizing the exact meaning of "mimesis" can thus be seen to be hopeless; Plato's entire attitude is in question, and not his use of one word or two words.[40]

Why is Plato's attitude split? Here we can only make suggestions; but one point that is helpful, I think, is to notice that he takes literature seriously. This may sound strange: Do not the two book 10 arguments show him taking poetry most *un*seriously? On their own they might; what matters more is that they try to prove the superficiality of what he elsewhere sees as far from superficial. Plato was himself, after all, a great literary artist, who did philosophy in a literary way; whatever we make of this when we study him philosophically, we cannot regard it as a fact of which he was unaware. And when he touches on poetry when it is not his main subject, he arguably shows an attitude that takes it more seriously than do those thinkers who are prepared to subordinate literature to other aims. (It is significant that by the time he wrote *What Is Art?* Tolstoy regarded his own literary past as something of an embarrassment.) When Plato discusses poetry tangentially, as he does in the *Ion, Meno,* and *Phaedrus,*[41] he describes the poet as a divinely inspired being; and I think we should take this seriously. Admittedly this notion is partly put forward to undermine the poet's cognitive claims; it goes with the idea that the poet lacks knowledge and at least in the *Ion* is the basis for some irony and mockery.[42] But the image of divine possession does underline one thing: The poet cannot compromise with the claims of the Muses. If he does, and composes to order, then he is not using his gift rightly. The image in the *Ion* of the poet as one link in a magnetic chain through which passes the power of a god[43] prepares us for the stronger language of the *Phaedrus:* "But if any man come to the gates of poetry without the madness of the Muses, persuaded that skill alone will make him a good poet, then shall he and his works of sanity with him be brought to naught by the poetry of madness, and, behold, their place is nowhere to be found."[44] As much as any Romantic, Plato believes that the true poet is born and not made.

This view of the poet leads to conflict when the poet's message can be found objectionable. Plato regards the creative writer as dangerous because he can be, or seem to be, a serious rival to the philosopher. The poet is more dangerous than the painter because the poet deals in the philosopher's own medium of words, and the poet's work has a cognitive content that people absorb in defiance of the philosopher's teaching, largely because poetry comes to them in a more attractive form. Plato pays the creative writer the compliment of regarding him as a serious rival; how serious, emerges in a remarkable passage from the *Laws,* where poet and philosopher are presented as rival writers of tragedy: " '. . . Our polity has all been framed in imitation of the best and fairest life; which, as for us, we hold to be in very truth the truest tragedy. Thus if you are poets, then we too are poets, makers of the selfsame things, rivals in your art, and rival actors in the finest of all dramas. . . . Do not imagine, then, that we shall ever with light heart allow you thus to plant your stage beside us in the market-place, or let you introduce your actors with melodious voices to drown our own, harangue the children, womenfolk, and all the crowd, about the same concerns as we do, and not say the same as we, but in the main and on most topics just the opposite. We should be absolutely mad if we did that' . . ."[45]

The creative writer who is not a philosopher is for Plato a serious and problematic rival. In book 3 Plato tries to disarm this rival and perhaps enlist him as an ally. In the final argument of book 10 he gives up that idea, but still regards him as a serious rival. But in the first two arguments of book 10 we find another response: We find

Plato trying to show that the poet does not *create* at all. He is merely a man with a mirror, doing something silly that requires no knowledge. So he cannot be seen as a serious alternative to the philosopher—not, that is, by anyone with a modicum of intellect. The whole point of the assimilation of poetry to painting, the source of the charges of triviality brought against it, is the denial to it of any creativity. Plato can afford to treat only of the banal case of "photographic realism" in painting, because he is not especially interested in painting; what matters is that at all costs, and however implausibly, the *poet* be shown to be no rival to the philosopher in the production of truth. If the poet *were* creative, then he would be the serious rival that he was seen as being in book 3, and the third argument of book 10. The split in Plato's thought is radical, but understandable if we take it to derive from the fact that he takes poetry seriously in a way that he does not extend to the visual arts. If the poet is truly creative, then he is a rival; Plato is split between accepting the fact of the poet's creativity and trying to cope with his rivalry, and the more desperate move of denying the poet any creativity at all and so eliminating him as a rival, reducing him to the time waster who mirrors the world.

If something like this is right, then any attempt to harmonize books 3 and 10 must be deeply misconceived. There need not have been, and perhaps never was, any such flatly representational painting (never mind poetry), as Plato is sometimes taken to be attacking in book 10. (Nor can he be attacking contemporary trends; as Collingwood pointed out long ago, the chief brunt of the attack falls on Homer.) Further, and more interestingly, the discussion of mimesis in book 10 is not a serious contribution to literary theory. Usually it is taken as Plato's most mature comment on poetry, and made the basis for the claim that he has an essentially imitative or mimetic theory of literature,[46] one to be contrasted with Aristotle's, where mimesis in introduced in terms of tragedy rather than painting. But if we think of mimesis in book 3, and the discussion of tragedy in book 10, rather than the forced analogy with painting, Plato's notion of mimesis looks rather more like Aristotle's than is commonly supposed. Briefly, and very speculatively, I would suggest that insofar as Plato has anything like a serious theory of the nature of poetry (one that can be gleaned from the *Ion, Phaedrus,* and the *Republic* apart from the notorious two arguments) it is not a mimetic but an expressive theory not unlike Aristotle's. But this is speculation; and I agree that Plato has made things difficult for us here.

Within the *Republic,* however, Plato's attitude is split, and he is not like the socialist realists, or Tolstoy, who think that it is both possible and necessary to throw out ephemeral, entertainment art and to promote deep, truth-promoting art. For to think this is to think that art and literature can be harnessed to a moral end while remaining themselves, genuinely creative. Plato does not consistently believe this. He does not really think that the poet's inspiration will tamely submit to the control and shaping of correct ideas. Because he does take poetry seriously, because he recognizes that the creative writer must answer only to the Muses' inspiration if he is not to deform his gift, Plato cannot in the end hold consistently that good art and poetry are what promote a moral end, however seriously he urges the need to reform ourselves to attain the moral end.

Plato may or may not have thought that his shocking two arguments in book 10 were good, convincing arguments. But we have good reason to be grateful for their presence, for by showing up the split in Plato's thought about poetry in the *Republic,* they show us that in spite of book 3 Plato cannot be considered the advocate of "civic poetry"; he knows that poetry if it is real cannot serve civic purposes, or at least cannot be depended to do so, and he knows that the verses he finally permits are not real poetry.[47] He thinks that poetry may always conflict with morality, and so he cannot be classed with those who think that poetry can and should serve morality, and that the fact that at present it does not do so is a temporary fault, correctible by political means that will produce a purified literature of the future. As often, Plato's thought is more uncompromising, and more pessimistic about the harmonious joint attainment of different kinds of good, than modern theories that we find more familiar and more congenial.

NOTES

1. *Laws* 669–70.

2. When he talks in book 3 about harmful stories and tales, Plato has in mind chiefly fables about the gods and what we would call fairytales. Cf.377a–c, where the censored and controlled stories are those told to children by nurses and mothers. *Logopoioi* are mentioned together with *poiétai* at 392a13, and the *muthologos* with the *poiétés* at 398b1, as having to submit to the regulation about both form and content of their *logoi te kai muthoi* (398b7); but Plato nowhere devotes concern to the style or form of prose works, as he does for music and poetry.

3. Possibly he would have taken something like Aristotle's view that history is concerned only with details of the particular. For Plato this would be, even if a source of enjoyment, potentially corrupting inasmuch as it encouraged us to spend our time paying attention to imperfect individual lives, instead of concentrating on how to improve the human condition in general. Plato would not welcome history just because it was true, rather than false or fictional. (See n. 4.)

4. Later, in the intriguing Atlantis story in the *Timaeus* and *Critias*, he does seem to take the notion of a fictional story seriously. See Christopher Gill, "The Genre of the Atlantis Story," *Classical Philology* (1977) (and cf. his "The Origin of the Atlantis Myth," *Trivium* (1976), and "Plato and Politics—the *Critias* and the *Politicus*," *Phronesis* [1979]). Gill relates the Atlantis story to Plato's remarks about falsity and fiction in the *Republic* in "Plato's Atlantis story and the Birth of Fiction," *Philosophy and Literature* (1979).

5. *Poiésis* (cf. 595a3) is to make her successful defense, if such is possible, "in lyric or other meter" (607d3–4). In the *Laws* (811–12, cf. 817b) the carefully worded regulations are held up, bizarrely, as a model for *poets*.

6. 401aff. Plato just asserts that painting, weaving, etc., have the same kind of effect as poetry. His general account of the effects of all the art forms tells us nothing as to which form is primary; the metaphor is of young animals grazing in good or unhealthy pastures.

7. The word is *spoudazein* (599a6–b1)

8. 599b3–7. Translations are from G. M. A. Grube's translation of the *Republic*, (Indianapolis, Ind.: Hackett Publishing Company, 1974).

9. This is Collingwood's view; cf. his "Plato's Philosophy of Art," *Mind* (1925), pp. 154–72, esp. p. 164: "The specialized and isolated form of aesthetic experience which we call *par excellence* the life of art is certainly by him excluded from the ideal state, as being no true element in the life of reason; but aesthetic experience as such remains for him a permanent and necessary part of the life of reason, insofar as that experience is modified or controlled by reason itself. As we have seen, art is not banished from the ideal state. It remains the great educative power by which the young guardians are to continue in the practice of it, in shapes suitable to their intellectual and moral status."

10. But here architecture is regularly a problem for general accounts of the arts. See R. Scruton, "Architectural Aesthetics," *British Journal of Aesthetics*, 1973 pp. 327–45, and "Architectural Taste," *British Journal of Aesthetics*, 1975, pp. 294–328.

11. Cf. *Nicomachean Ethics*, book 2, chs. 1–3. We become just by doing just acts, and we have to begin by doing what the just man would do, without full understanding and taking a lot on trust—by imitating the just man, in fact. Aristotle too seems to be committed to the idea that if we imitate many conflicting "role

models" (in the modern phrase) we will end up with an incoherent moral character—something that seems to be true.

12. This *is* surprising, given 595a3–5—*peri poieseós . . . to médaméi paradechesthai autés hosé mimétiké.* We expect the discussion to concern poetry alone.

13. Collingwood, for example (op. cit., p. 155) says that in spite of the discussion being introduced as concerning poetry, the sequel shows that Plato is fully aware of "the substantial identity of nature which unites poetry with painting." But this is to grant Plato his strange claim before the argument begins.

14. G. Else, *Aristotle's Poetics: The Argument* (Cambridge, Mass.: Harvard University Press, 1957), p. 27.

15. *Republic* 533c–d.

16. The man containing a little man, a lion, and a weird protean beast, at *Republic* 588c–d; the talk of the birth of babies and of destroyable "windeggs" in the *Theaetetus;* one might add the whole Sun, Line, and Cave sequence in the *Republic,* where it is notoriously impossible to give a single overall interpretation that is both visually and philosophically coherent.

17. 401aff gives us a distinction between good and bad painting; and there are the passages where the work of the philosopher is compared to that of a painter who is clearly doing more than merely copy mindlessly. Cf. 420c, 472d, 484c, 500–1.

18. Though even so, surely Plato is not right in taking the *aim* of *trompe-l'oeil* painting to be the actual deception. Surely the aim is to elicit admiration for the skill that can produce a likeness good enough to deceive on occasion; this pleasure can be felt repeatedly, whereas one could only be deceived by the painting once. Veronese's frescoes at the Villa Maser include *trompe-l'oeil* figures of members of the family, their cat, dog, etc., which were presumably never intended to produce an illusion of reality, but merely to be enjoyed for their skill. (No doubt Plato would despise this aim also, but it is not the one he actually attributes.)

19. *Apology* 22a–c. The *Ion* is devoted to undermining the *rhapsode's* claim to knowledge, but in the process Plato represents the poet as suffering the same kind of deficiency (536aff).

20. Here I shall touch on, without going adequately into, the important point that this passage of the *Republic* seems to think of knowledge as a kind of justified true belief—at any rate as being true belief *plus* some factor. This fits with the passages at *Meno* 97ff and *Theaetetus* 200–1, which also take knowledge to be a kind of belief rendered especially firm and unshakeable. Such a concept of knowledge does not require that the *objects* of knowledge be special—that they be Forms, for example—and in all three of these passages we find it said that we can have knowledge of particular things or facts. This does not fit with the account of knowledge prominent in the *Republic*'s central books, where the objects of knowledge are necessarily distinct from those of belief, and where, at the end of book 5, Plato constructs an argument around our confident intuitions about what knowledge is, with belief as the problematic item that has to be constructed by subtraction from knowledge.

21. The difficulties here are clearly brought out in Appendix B to ch. 11 of N. Murphy's *The Interpretation of Plato's Republic* (Oxford: Clarendon Press, 1959), pp. 239–43.

22. I owe the idea in this paragraph to a paper by Cass Weller.

23. There is another difficulty—namely, how *either* of the divisions of the soul here fit with that made in book 4 (to which Plato seems to be appealing in using a principle of opposition to establish distinct parts, and referring to its earlier use [602e]). But as used in book 4 that principle seemed to contrast reason with desire thought of as lacking any beliefs about its object (not that this is Plato's considered

view throughout the *Republic*). But the conflict in the soul created by visual illusions is a conflict in beliefs, clearly described as such (602e8–9); and the lower part to which poetry appeals has opinions, if wrong ones, about the relative values of things (603c–d, 604d). On the other hand, the worthless part is called "far from reason" (603a12) and "mindless" (605b9). The difficulties are compounded by the fact that it is hard to see how the third part of the soul, the *thumoeides*, is to fit in. It has no place in the case of optical illusions, and in the discussion of the conflict of reason and the part to which poetry appeals, its roles seem to be partitioned between the two factors distinguished there. The rational part in fighting grief and sorrow obeys "law" (604b) in a way making the rational principle seem external as it is for the spirited part. On the other hand, the emotions that have to be resisted, like grief, seem conceptually as complex as anger and not very like desire.

24. 597e6–8, 598e5–599b7, 599d2–e7, 600e4–601b4, 602b6–c2, 605a8–c4.

25. Most readers of the *Republic* probably feel that book 10 is not an organic part of the whole book, but arguments to make this convincing are hard to come by. For a perverse but stimulating discussion of book 10 see G. Else, *The Structure and Date of Book 10 of Plato's Republic* (Heidelberg, 1972).

26. I shall refer to the Aylmer Maude translation in the volume *What Is Art? and Essays on Art* (New York: Oxford University Press, 1929).

27. Op. cit., pp. 265–66. New York.

28. Chernyshevsky's works will be cited from the translation, N. G. Chernyshevsky, *Selected Philosophical Essays,* Moscow: Foreign Languages Publishing House, 1950–51. Good accounts of Chernyshevsky's aesthetics can be found in the relevant chapters of E. Lampert, *Sons Against Fathers* (Oxford: Clarendon Press, 1965), F. B. Randall, *N. G. Chernyshevskii* (New York: Twayne Publishers, 1967), W. F. Woehrlin, *Chernyshevskii: the Man and the Journalist* (Cambridge, Mass.: Harvard University Press, 1971), N. G. O. Pereira, *The Thought and Teachings of N. G. Černyševkij,* (The Hague, Paris: Mouton, 1975). Chernyshevsky reviewed and admired Tolstoy; see Randall, pp. 59–63.

29. See J. P. Scanlan, "Can Realism be Socialist?," *British Journal of Aesthetics* (1974), pp. 41–55.

30. See J. P. Scanlan, "The Impossibility of a Uniquely Authentic Marxist Aesthetics," *British Journal of Aesthetics* (1976), pp. 128–36.

31. For Mill's critical work, see M. H. Abrams, *The Mirror and the Lamp* (New York: Oxford University Press, 1953), pp. 23–26. It is highly interesting that for Abrams Mill serves as a good example of "the revolution in critical norms" toward the Romantic stress on the poet's expression of his state of mind and away from the importance of representation of the world. Mill stresses spontaneity; makes lyric poetry the best example of poetry and treats plot in epic and drama as secondary; and makes the poet's relation to an audience, and his depiction of the world, merely aspects of his own self-expression. All this is completely antithetical to a utilitarian outlook on poetry, and stresses how little utilitarian Mill's personal sensibility was.

32. *Selected Philosophical Essays*, p. 376; this comes, like the quotation below, from Chernyshevsky's earliest and most influential work on aesthetics, his doctoral dissertation "The Aesthetic Relation of Art to Reality."

33. P. 368. He developed the point at greater length in a long review of a Russian translation of Aristotle's *Poetics* by B. Ordynsky *(Selected Philosophical Essays,* pp. 422–53.)

34. Though on this it is worth reading Nabokov's novel *The Gift*, a self-conscious and relentlessly "literary" attack on the whole idea that art has anything to do with social purpose. Chapter 4 of the novel is a malicious and deadly short

biography of Chernyshevsky written by the novel's hero, summing up all Nabokov's hostility to everything Chernyshevsky represents. Because of Chernyshevsky's great moral prestige, the chapter is rejected by a Russian emigré magazine in the novel; and ironically so it was in fact. It was published only twenty years
later. Pereira, p. 90, calls it "defamatory"; the way it has divided people shows up
quite well the shape of the modern conflict between the claims of the autonomy of
art and the claim that art must have a social purpose.

35. Hence his (reciprocated) hostility to Turgenev, and his famous dismissal of
the latter's story *Asya*: "Forget about these erotic questions! They are not for the
reader of our times, preoccupied with the problems of improving the bureaucracy
and the judiciary, with reforming the finances, and with the emancipation of the
serfs!" For Chernyshevsky it is morally lax to spend the time and effort examining
one's own ineffective feelings the way Turgenev does. See Randall, pp. 63–69. In
this respect Nabokov can be seen as Turgenev's heir (see n. 34).

36. Op. cit., p. 320. This has become "the most quoted idea of his whole
aesthetics" (Randall, p. 47); rather like Plato's discussion of paintings of beds and
tables, it has led to exaggeration of the crudity of his approach.

37. The discussion at 396c–397e is very confusing. What is to be admitted into
the ideal state is only the "unmixed" style. The way in which this was introduced
suggested that it was nonimitative; but we find that it will include some imitation,
though not much, and only of the good man. We can conclude that Plato finds it hard
to make his mind up here. this seems to me more plausible than the view of J. Tate
(" 'Imitation' in Plato's *Republic*," *Classical Quarterly* [1928], p. 18), who refers to
this as "the unmixed style which imitates the virtuous man . . . in other words, (1)
the nonimitative style, which nevertheless contains such kinds of imitation as the
virtuous poet will not disdain to practice." We should require explicit warning
before saddling Plato with a nonimitative style that is, all the same, imitative.

38. Cf. the article by Tate cited in n. 37; also his "Plato and Imitation," *Classical
Quarterly* (1932), and "Plato, Art, and Mr. Maritain," *The New Scholasticism*
(1938); L. Golden, "Plato's Concept of Mimesis," *British Journal of Aesthetics*
(1975); D. Grey, "Art in the *Republic*," *Philosophy* (1952).

39. In the *Republic* the analogue is the painter (cf. references in n. 17); in the
Laws it is the poet (cf. references in n. 5).

40. For a discussion of the background to Plato here, see G. F. Else, "Imitation
in the Fifth Century," *Classical Philology* (1958), pp. 73–90. Results of philological
inquiry seem to me to be likely to be of little help, since Plato (and Aristotle) is
clearly using the word for his own purposes, in a theoretical framework.

41. *Meno* 99c–d; *Ion* 533d–534e (cf. esp. 534b), 536a–d, *Phaedrus* 245a.

42. In the *Ion* the mockery is aimed at Ion, the stupid rhapsode; it is not clear
how much is meant to carry over to the poet. Perhaps Plato thinks that the poet
might be as stupid as Ion is and still be an excellent poet, just as Ion is uncontrover-
sially an excellent rhapsode.

43. *Ion* 533d–534e, 536a–d.

44. *Phaedrus* 245a, Hackforth's translation (Cambridge: Cambridge University
Press, 1952).

45. *Laws* 817b (Lane Cooper translation).

46. I take the terms "mimetic" and "expressive" from Abrams' discussion (see
n. 31); but I am conscious that the present remarks are extremely sketchy and little
but a promissory note.

47. The notorious "hymns to the gods and eulogies of good men" cannot but stir
suggestions of ludicrous and toadying "state poetry" of the kind composed in the

futuristic kind of society described in Zamyatin's *We*, where poets celebrate the execution of "state criminals." But Plato is not, I think, assigning to poetry even an important propaganda role; the poetry he finally allows is meant to be insignificant.

CHAPTER II
Noetic Aspiration and Artistic Inspiration
Julius Moravcsik

As the *Symposium* shows, the ancient Greeks—like most other groups in the history of our culture—assumed that there are some dominant motives, drives, or interests that determine the major aims in human lives. Discussions about what the dominant motive in life should be centered around the notion of eros. Some conceptions of eros interpreted it as the drive to satisfy physical appetites, while others took it to be the inspiration of love. Plato's conception of eros was very different from either of these views.[1] He thought that once the human condition was properly understood, the dominant eros of a human life must be the aspiration toward theoretical insight and understanding.[2] There are two reasons why Plato thought that this kind of understanding has to be the dominant aim in a well-lived life. First, he thought that the achievement of such understanding is the only state that is intrinsically satisfying without leading to further needs and to the demand for the supply of additional external goods. Second, he thought that only this kind of understanding leads to real freedom, for in this state a human is free from the constraints that exclusive preoccupation with empirical matters places upon the unreflective.

Self-knowledge is a necessary condition of freedom, for it is the awareness of what we believe and why that opens up the possibilities for considering new alternatives. Self-knowledge, however, requires—according to Plato—theoretical understanding: It becomes possible only after we analyzed human nature in terms of its relationships to the Forms, in particular the Forms that embody the excellences.

These are, then, the reasons why in a well-lived life noetic aspiration has to be the mainspring for all of our activities. What

Plato says about art and beauty has to be seen in light of these considerations.

It is well known that Plato contrasts the conception of human well-being dominated by noetic aspiration with hedonistic and relativistic schemes, apparently popular in Athens in Plato's time. It is less well known that Plato contrasts his conception also with one that places high premium on inspiration, in particular the inspiration and accompanying sensitivities that are associated with the production and enjoyment of literature and the fine arts.

The main theme of this chapter is that according to Plato while the objects and products of noetic aspiration are intrinsically good, the objects and products of inspiration have at best instrumental value insofar as they contribute to the seeking of understanding on higher, more theoretical levels. At their worst they lead us astray, since they suggest the self-contained nature of art and its allegedly intrinsically meritorious insights, and hence keep us from reaching toward the kind of understanding that culminates in the contemplation of the Forms. For Plato a poem has to be either useful for the care of the soul—as the products of the physician are for the care of the body—or be there purely for pleasure. He does not allow for a third possibility, which is to say that in his conceptual scheme there is no room for a special capacity for aesthetic understanding and enjoyment, such as the one we mark in modern philosophic discourse by the expression "taste." This can be brought out by contrasting the views of Plato and Aristotle with the view embodied in Kant's *Critique of Judgment*.

The contrast between aspiration and inspiration, as well as the lack of the concept of taste, help us also to understand why Plato can denounce poetry and literature (for example, in *Republic* 595a,b) and then employ so many poetic and literary devices in his own writings. This will become clearer as this exposition proceeds.

It may seem odd that so much is written on Plato's conceptions of beauty and art when, in fact, there are no separate words for "beauty" and "art," respectively, in the Greek prose of Plato's time. Needless to say, Plato can describe in other words the phenomena that we gather today under the labels of "beauty" and "art." Thus, for example, he talks of appreciating the appearance of bodies as well as appreciating poetry; and he discusses the ingredients of the arts of poets and painters.

One can possess a concept even if it is not marked in the language by a special word. For example, a speaker of English may have the concept of a special kind of snow even if it is not marked in the English lexicon the way it is in certain Eskimo languages. One can repair such lacunae without causing major disturbances in one's conceptual scheme.

But the situation we are confronting here is more complicated than the mere absence of a word or two from the dictionary. As *Symposium* 210–12 shows, what seems to correspond to our notion of beauty is regarded by Plato as a species of a genus called *kalon*. Even a cursory glance at a lexicon like that of Liddell and Scott shows that this word is applied in nonphilosophic prose and literary use to actions, currency, precious metal, and wine, as well as to the appearances of persons. It always has a nonfunctional and nonutilitarian connotation. Hence the best translation is the English word "fine," and what we call beautiful is for the Greeks "fine in appearance." There is, however, another assumption built into Plato's use of *kalon*, one that he did not share with his contemporaries, for the implications of Plato's use include the claim that insofar as an object is beautiful, it is fine "*merely* in appearance." This pejorative connotation was not shared by Plato's contemporaries. It presupposes Plato's view of reality according to which things do not wear their essences on their sleeves. In other words, excellence in appearance does not indicate much, if anything, about the true nature of an entity. In this respect, however, Plato's conception does not reflect what is built into the Greek equivalent of "appearance"; the metaphysical pioneer goes beyond the common sense of his contemporaries.

Thus while for the average Athenian calling something fine in appearance would not amount to associating an object with a low-grade species of what is fine, for Plato the designation not only places the beautiful within the larger scheme of the fine, but also assigns to it a low status within this field. Since the ability to grasp mere appearances cannot lead, according to Plato, to adequate understanding, the appreciation of beauty cannot lead to real understanding.

Thus mere reflection on Greek usage, together with some of Plato's views on understanding and on the structure of reality give us the main outlines of his views on beauty. (Argumentative readers have been wanting to say, no doubt for some time, that in modern—colloquial—usage we employ expressions like "the beauty of this proof," or "this beautiful person," uses that do not mark aesthetic qualities. In these respects modern American uses of "beautiful" are beginning to approximate some of the nonaesthetic uses of the Greek *kalon*.)

The relationship between the Greek word *techne* and the word "art," which is used most frequently in translations, introduces further complexities. "Art" has a process-product ambiguity; hence a theory of art can be either an account of the artistic creative process, or an account of the essential features of entities that we label "works of art." (These accounts can be interrelated.) *Techne,* however, does not indicate either process or product; it designates, rather, the skill, knowhow, or knowledge that a practitioner in any of the acknowledged professions must possess. Hence the naturalness of the Platonic question, "What is a *techne* used for?"—a question that is not equivalent either to the question, "What is the artistic process used for?" or to the question, "What is a work of art used for?"

Furthermore, the *techne* of an artist is viewed as a species among the *technai* of other professions—those of craftsmen, lawgivers, physicians, etc. This is the context, both in the *Gorgias* and in such later dialogues as the *Sophist* and *Politicus,* within which the various professions are discussed. The dominant question is: How does any given *techne* enable one to contribute to the welfare of human beings? Given Plato's view that his *techne* enables the artist to have insight only into the structure of appearances, and that appearances do not tell us much about the essences of things, one cannot expect to find in Plato a very high ranking of this particular skill, even—as we shall see—in its inspired form.

Our brief investigation into the relevant lexical matters suggests that questions about beauty should be treated separately from questions about art. This suggestion will seem strange only to those who are corrupted by the modern word "aesthetics" and phrase "aesthetic theory," terms that are used to bring under one label both theories about what makes an object beautiful—and the corresponding appreciation—as well as theories about what makes something a work of art, and what it takes to appreciate such products. In this sense, neither Plato nor Aristotle had "aesthetic theories." They saw, rightly, that questions about beauty and its enjoyment are separate from questions about what a work of art is, and what it takes to appreciate art.

Our daily lives provide countless examples to show that the appreciation of beauty cannot be identified with the appreciation of art. A small child takes delight in many objects on account of their aesthetic qualities, without even having the concept of a work of art. Adults too take delight in objects other than works of art, such as the beauty of nature or that of other persons. Hence the features that render something beautiful cannot be identical with the features that make something a work of art; thus the enjoyment of beauty cannot be identical with the appreciation of art.

Facts suggesting the same separation come to mind when one reflects on our treatment of works of art. Though being beautiful is one of the criteria that we invoke when assessing the merits of some works of art, there are many other criteria, such as creativity, novelty, originality, magnitude of achievement, etc. Thus neither the artist nor his product "lives by beauty alone." These same considerations show how complex the appreciation of art is. The ability to appreciate beauty is only one of the many prerequisites. People who cannot admire originality, creativity, etc., are not able to appreciate this special (and, apparently, all-pervasive) human capacity—that is, the capacity to produce objects that delight us, and occasionally move us, in constantly changing novel patterns.

I

A Portrait of the Artist. In the middle books of the *Republic* Plato presents his account of what a good human should be like. The ingredients of this analysis are: function, motivation, required skill and understanding, and expected effects. Plato's portrait of the artist in *Republic* book 10, and the relevant sections of the *Phaedrus,* mirror this structure. Furthermore, the same structure governs his accounts of other skills and professions, such as those of the physician or mathematician. It would never occur to Plato to question the legitimacy of this structure. He assumes that any rational discussion of healing, mathematics, teaching, etc., will have to specify what the effects of physicians, teachers, mathematicians, etc., should be both on society in general and on particular individuals. Likewise, he assumes that a discussion of the artist must include suggestions of what the effects of the artist on society are and should be.

In some well-known passages (for example, *Republic* 10, 603a10–c8), Plato states that the products of the artist are representations of sensible objects or qualities, and that the artist's main function is to please and move people with these products. As these passages show, Plato's notion of "representation" has to be taken in a very wide sense; it includes the representation of sounds and colors also, not only the representation of material objects. Hence the account applies not only to what in modern times we call representational art, but also to what is called "nonrepresentational art" in painting, sculpture, and literature. In all of these cases what is represented is something particular and sensible, hence something that is ontologically posterior to the Forms.

The claim that the artist pleases and moves people is hardly controversial. What makes Plato's claim controversial is that he does not see anything special about the way in which the artist pleases or moves people. The artist appears as merely one of the many "pleasure producers."

These considerations help us to see much of Aristotle's *Poetics* as a series of comments on Plato. For example, Aristotle's views on *katharsis* are qualifications on Plato's conception of the artist as a pleasure producer. Aristotle agrees that the function of drama is to affect us, but he thinks that drama does this in a special way.

In stating that the artist moves, Plato underlines the fact that our response to art is not merely intellectual. This by itself is not objectionable in Plato's eyes. But in his view, the proper way to move humans is to affect the emotions only through the exercise of understanding. The artist fails to meet this requirement. Furthermore, given this fact and the Platonic dichotomy of either pleasing people or caring for their welfare, it follows that in his primary function the artist does not contribute to the care of the souls of the audience.

Can the artist fulfill his function regardless of the mental state he is in? The question of the proper state of mind, or motivation, is raised by Plato not only in connection with the artist. In discussing the physician Plato points out that *qua* physician the practitioner has to be altruistic and concern himself solely with the welfare of the patient (for example, *Republic* 346c–e). For reasons that should be clear by now, Plato does not say that about the artist. Still, if not in terms of function or the nature of the product, at least in terms of the required state of mind, Plato distinguishes the artist from the other pleasure producers, for in discussing the various types of divine *mania,* or inspiration, Plato includes (*Phaedrus* 245a2–b1) that which the poet possesses (mere *mania* is best rendered as "madness," while divine *mania* is equivalent, roughly, to "inspiration"). In this passage Plato insists that only the inspired artist can be a good artist. Only in that state does he or she have the kind of sensitivity that enables the artist to produce a moving work of art. At no point, however, is inspiration construed as a special kind of insight; the inspired poet still lacks what Plato would regard as genuine knowledge or understanding. But at least in the inspired state the artist is not looking out merely for his own pleasure; he is—in Plato's view—between the pleasure seeking of the *hoi polloi* and the altruism of the true physician, statesman, or teacher. Hence he or she can experience things that humans in their ordinary sober state cannot.

We saw already that for Plato the true "erotic" person regards all stages of life as pointing toward the understanding of the Forms, with the accompanying freedom and self-determination. This erotic and noetic aspiration clashes with the inspiration of the artist. The inspired artist does not regard her work as pointing beyond itself, to higher levels of understanding. According to her, poetic inspiration and insight is the highest, or at least one of the highest levels of human attainment. We shall see later how this clash helps to explain the difference between the Platonically "good" and "bad" works of art.

The inspired artist has skill and knowledge of the means that he or she uses. But since understanding human nature, or, for that matter, the nature of sounds (*Philebus* 17d–e) requires abstract and theoretic understanding—of which mathematics is for Plato a paradigm instance—the artist in the Platonic scheme is presented as lacking adequate understanding of the nature of the objects to be represented.

This sounds harsh and unfair to the modern ear. One might say that even if we grant that Homer was no expert on warfare, strategy, etc., there are features of war that he knew as much about, if not more, than any general. The grasp of these features—for example, the cruelty and senselessness of war—requires not practical knowledge of the useful or instrumental, nor theoretical grasp of a priori laws, but certain kinds of sensitivity. Capacities for such sensitivity are precisely what poets and their appreciators are likely to have more of than the average person.

At this point we run up against one of the cornerstones of Plato's epistemology and ethics, for there is no room in Plato's scheme for sensitivities that are not based on understanding. Though Plato does not discuss these, his classifications commit him to relegating them to the same low status at which other capacities based on mere *empeiria* stand. Homer may have been a pioneer in giving expression to compassion for the many who died senselessly in the Trojan war, and Neoptolemus may be represented as having the insight that at times kindness is more important than expediency and loyalty to the army. But there is no room within Plato's scheme of excellences for the acknowledgment of such insights. Attitudes formed on the basis of understanding outrank mere sensitivity.

This is one of the extreme consequences of Plato's rationalism. Perhaps one can see still another of Aristotle's claims in the *Poetics* as an attempt to modify this austere view. Aristotle agrees with his master that the object of understanding must be universal, but leaves room for insight reached via dramatic representation when he sees the dramatist as representing the universal in the particular.

Still, even if one accepts extreme rationalism, could not Plato appreciate drama in which wisdom prevails? Why could not plays like *The Tempest* or *Faust* qualify? Could it be that Plato is not aware of the possibility of such drama? In order to see that this will not do, we need to reflect merely on the a priori character of Platonic wisdom, the character that precludes its originating in experience. On this point Plato opposes one of the key dicta of Greek drama, one that applies to *The Tempest* and *Faust* as well. It is embodied in the well-known motto, *Too pathei mathos* (roughly, "We learn through [suffering] experience"). One of Plato's penetrating insights is the claim that literature can portray only the kind of wisdom that is gained through experience. Progression through dialectic and mathematical training does not offer dramatic material.

Apart from disputes about the merits of artistic insight, Plato's portrait of the artist lacks conspicuously—by modern standards—in emphasis on originality and creativity, traits associated in modern times very closely with the artist. But if this is negligence, it can be found not only in Plato's portrait of the artist, but in his portraits of the scientists and philosophers as well. This lack of high esteem for creativity does not have its roots in some deep yearning for the unchanging. Rather, the roots lie in Plato's conception of adequate understanding and the sciences. For him mathematics is not a matter of constructions and creations, but a matter of discovering antecedently given timeless relationships between the Forms. Arriving at the truth is for Plato a matter of discovery rather than that of creation. Hence creativity has at most instrumental rather than intrinsic value.

Finally, we come to the effects of art. Plato's insistence that art moves and is taken by people as providing insight into life is not a normative claim but rather a claim about what is in fact true in all human cultures (*Republic* 601b1–4, 605a2–6, 605c10–d5). Plato is not forcing a didactic interpretation on art. He simply acknowledges a role that literature plays in all cultures. Since art has this effect, Plato feels justified in asking whether this effect is beneficial. Since the only beneficial effects are those that lead away from the sensible and the concrete and toward the abstract and the universal, we can see why Plato cannot give art high marks on that score.[3]

This is, then, Plato's portrait of the artist—inspired, sensitive, skillful, but lacking in rational insight and in aspiration for the only type of understanding whose possession Plato regarded as the proper end of a well-lived human life. Creative and imaginative maybe, but lacking the noetic foundation on the basis of which the artist could offer reliable guidance for life, and lacking the selfless concern for the welfare of others that Plato does not deduce from some categorical imperative, but construes as an attitude formed naturally by those—like the true physician—who have an understanding of human nature and its potential for excellence.

II

The Product. Plato places the product "third removed" from what he regards as most fundamental in reality (*Republic* 597e3–4). Given the nature of the Forms for artifacts, this is a metaphysical correlate of what we have been saying about the different competences required of the physician and the craftsman on the one hand, and the artist on the other, for the Forms for artifacts are whatever correspond in reality to functional specifications (*Republic* 601d4–6). Hence these Forms are neither perfect particulars of some sort, nor what would correspond in reality to definitions in terms of structural specifications. The manifestations of, for example, goodness, will vary depending on social and personal contexts. In the same way, the structural properties of a good bed will vary depending on the cultural, technological, and social context in which the craftsman produces it. As Plato says, the craftsman must know what a bed is used for in order to produce what is under the circumstances the most appropriate object answering the functional specifications.

These reflections explain also why Plato does not discuss the individuation of Forms for artifacts. It is important for a science like mathematics that the domain it deals with—the domain of numbers—should be well ordered. But functional specifications overlap. Hence the senselessness of the question, How many Forms for the different artifacts does Plato's theory require?

The epistemological consequence of these views of Plato is that the artist does not have an adequate grasp of the functional specifications, and thus of a vital part of the nature, of the objects that he represents. This is the main reason why Plato objects to the artist's lack of concern with the "invisible" or nonsensible. His objection is not simply a dogmatic insistence that we must seek the nonempirical. That insistence follows rather from the more directly relevant point that artistic representations are not linked to functional values. The point applies across the different art forms. The painter, musician, and poet-dramatist are equally ignorant of the function and purpose of the objects that represent. This claim cuts deeper than the charge that the dramatist is a mere pleasure producer. It is difficult to dismiss, for example, Sophocles as a mere pleasure producer; but it is true that neither do Sophocles' insights lead to the kind of theory of human nature that Plato seeks, nor could one base Sophocles' portraits on Plato's analysis of the ingredients of the human psyche.

Plato regards the lack of understanding of function and purpose of the objects represented as a flaw in the artist, and hence a blemish expressed also in the products. Within this austere scheme, since the enjoyment of the product cannot teach the audience something about the important human potential, it must be inferior to the many objects that humans produce with an eye on the useful and beneficial. The nonfunctional nature of the work of art is recognized also by Kant. He, however, draws from this very different conclusions. According to Kant, the artist's mind is freed from the demands of the practical, and the rules of the necessary or a priori. Hence Kant can describe a work of art as "production through freedom" (*Critique of Judgment* No. 43). For Plato the requirement that significant creation should be informed by the practical is not a constraint, but an enabling condition. Hence Kant's freedom is Plato's constraint.

The relegation of works of art to the "third level" of reality brings out again the difference between Plato's treatment of works of art and his treatment of beauty, for some beautiful objects—for example, certain parts of nature—are not on the "third" level. Their beauty is due to direct participation in the Form of beauty. For example, in *Phaedrus* 250b–d Plato emphasizes that the Fine has sensible instances. A painting of a couch can partake of beauty, but is twice removed from the Form of being a couch.

Still, in some cases the artist can succeed in representing something good and fine. As Plato puts it (*Republic* 600e5–6), in these cases the artists represent images of excellence. Again, in *Phae-*

drus 245a2–5 Plato mentions the good that an artist's representation of the deeds of the ancients can do. But this too must be taken in the context of the major contrast between inspiration and aspiration. Only if these images are indeed viewed as mere images—that is, as leading us toward things that are on a higher ontological plane—can the artist's representations play a useful role. This conception of the product is entirely opposed to the one illustrated by the quotation above from Kant. If art—even "good" art,—captures our rapt attention and does not move us to go beyond it, and seek understanding on higher levels, then Plato regards its enjoyment as harmful to our souls. In this Plato opposes also the general conception of art that prevailed in the Athens of his time. The intrinsic value of the "fine things" and their enjoyment are lauded in such nonphilosophical texts as Pericles' Funeral Oration (Thucydides II. 38, 40).

The successful literary work of art portrays primarily the manifestations of passion and emotion (*Republic* 604d–e). Plato would acknowledge the difference between the treatment of emotions in a play like *Medea* and one like *Nathan der Weise*. But even where emotion is tempered by reason, the harmonious relationship in such plays is the result of learning through experience, rather than theoretical understanding; hence it cannot lead to Platonic enlightenment. This explains why there can be no philosophic drama. A philosophically good person's meeting misfortune would not be a tragedy; it would merely be sad or outrageous, for given the personality structure of the philosophically good person, there may be shortcoming but no tragic flaw in such an individual. Plato admits in *Republic* 604e that the *phronimos* (intelligent person) can be the object of representation, though the achievement of such representation seems to Plato difficult. But Plato does not say that such representation could be achieved within drama; in drama action is the dominant theme, in a representation of the *phronimos* thought has to occupy the center stage.

These considerations explain the apparent anomaly in the structure of the *Phaedo*. In the drama of the death of the wisest man that Plato knew, the center stage has to be filled with theories about the Forms and the nature of the soul. Only in the last scene does Plato allow the artist to emerge from within himself and to paint an unforgettable picture of courage and resignation—all of which, he wants us so desperately to believe, must come from nonempirical understanding rather than from the training of sensitivities that suffering experience can provide.

III

The Audience and the Missing Concept of Taste. We saw that the class of works of art do not form for Plato a separate ontological category. Likewise, when it comes to the discussion of enjoyment, the reaction of the audience is placed side by side with the experience of other types of enjoyment, experiences that Plato associates with the third (lowest) part of the soul.

What would it have taken for Plato to have recognized a separate capacity of taste, and thus of special enjoyment? In *Republic* V, 477c–d, he expounds his view about mental capacities. The positing of such a capacity depends on two factors; one of these is the existence of a special set of objects for this *dunamis,* and the other is a special achievement that the exercise of this capacity can bring about. On the basis of this scheme, Plato distinguishes knowledge from mere belief. An aesthetic capacity would have to have its own special set of objects, and its exercise would have to have a unique achievement or result. Plato's way of distinguishing capacities is notable also for what it does not say. It does not rely on using direct experience—introspective or behavioral—as the basis for establishing separateness claims. Hence it commits Plato to the view that the fundamental cognitive capacities—at least as far as their essential ingredients are concerned—can be studied only indirectly, through their objects and functions.

Kant's characterization of taste would fit the Platonic mold perfectly. Since when judging an object to be beautiful we do not subsume it under a concept, beauty remains a unique object of thought for Kant. Furthermore, his characterization of disinterested delight singles out a unique function for aesthetic enjoyment.

One need not agree with all of what Kant says about taste in order to agree with the main contention—that is, that aesthetic enjoyment is neither the result of interest in the useful, nor the mere recording of pleasant sensations. We need a way to separate the connoisseur from the glutton. Yet it is not clear how Plato's conceptual scheme allows him to do that. He can distinguish the poet from the cookie producer on the basis of the theory of *mania* of the *Phaedrus,* and in that respect this dialogue adds to the relevant material of the *Republic.* But he cannot draw an analogous line with respect to the audience or enjoying agent. The "good" audience is one that moves from the enjoyment of art to other "higher" objects. Modern artists would hardly thank Plato for allowing such a class of "good spectators." But the ones that the modern artist would prefer are relegated by Plato to the class of the "lovers of sights and sounds" (*Republic* 475d). The possibility of a Platonically "good" audience is responsible for the small positive role that Plato leaves for art to play in the educational scheme (*Republic* 377b, c, 522a). Finally, as we saw above, the argument that exposure to art can help develop sensitivity to examples of kindness, compassion, etc., would carry little weight with Plato, since he does not have room for such sensitivity in his scheme of excellences.

According to Kant, the exercise of taste involves reacting to an object on account of some of its unique qualities. It does not commit one to generalizations of this sort: "If I ever encounter again an object with qualities Q' . . . Q^n, then I will admire it." In his insistence that art and its appreciation can deal only with the particular, Plato seems to be tacitly accepting this view. Hence the contrast with "real" understanding that must have something general as its object. This is already at the heart of the "ladder of aspiration" expounded in *Symposium* 210–12. Plato's failure to accord a special place to beauty has the same conceptual roots as his failure to accord high position to any attitude that involves loyalty to an individual, regardless of changing characteristics. Friendship and love—as the *Phaedrus* shows—must involve, for Plato, commitment to some higher aim, and thus affection is conditional upon the continued acceptance of this aim. Compassion cannot be a Platonic virtue, nor can it be a virtue to be an audience that enjoys inspired creation for its own sake.

IV

Beauty Again. Some of Plato's main theses about beauty appeared already in our discussions of other topics. We saw that an instance of beauty need not be "third removed" from highest reality. We saw also that beauty is "fineness in appearance"—that is, a lower species of *kalon,* or the Fine. Thus when fully understood, not only in terms of what instances it can have, but also in terms of its place within the higher genus, beauty should lead us to the contemplation of things that are fine not only in appearance. At its worst, the appreciation of beauty can mire us in the world of sense experience (it helps us to lose our wings, as the *Phaedrus* would express it); but at its best it can lead to the understanding of goodness.

As we saw, this conception of beauty, as a notion to be leading us away from itself, did not correspond to the popular conception of beauty at Plato's time. Yet he could account for what would have been regarded as judgments of beauty according to the ordinary (vulgar) conception, just as he can account for the concept of courage of the *hoi polloi* in *Phaedo* 68d–69b. There he distinguishes real from merely apparent courage. To have merely apparent courage is to perform courageous acts for the wrong reasons—fear, vanity, etc. Thus we have the corresponding notion of unreflective judgments of courage—that is, ones based merely on behavior. The same distinction can be applied to judgments of fineness. The *hoi polloi* judge what is fine merely in terms of appearances. Thus they see beauty only in terms of appearances, not discerning its relationship to other aspects of the Fine, the ones that depend on the nonapparent essential qualities of things.

In Plato's theory there is no "autonomy of ethics." The discovery of the appropriate norms for healthy living depends on the formulation of the proper aims for human lives, and this, in turn, depends on an adequate understanding of human nature. By analogous reasoning, there is no room in Plato's philosophy for the "autonomy of aesthetics." The proper appreciation of what is fine in appearance involves seeing this characteristic as related to other characteristics, the discovery of which leads us to the understanding of the Forms. For Plato being beautiful and appreciating beauty are some of the lesser functions that constitute healthy living. The products of inspiration are subordinated to the products of aspiration.

These reflections help us to understand how Plato can denounce literature and poetry and at the same time employ literary and poetic devices in his own exposition of philosophy. Plato never uses simile or metaphor, or myth, unless the preferred method of exposition—rational, deductive argument and definition—is not available. When forced to use literary images, Plato always apologizes and indicates that this is only the second-best way to explain serious matters (for example, in the introduction to the chariot image *Phaedrus* 246a, and the introduction to the Sun simile *Republic* 507a). He thinks that we should use poetic images in philosophy the way mathematicians should use diagrams in their demonstrations. The function of both simile and diagram is to lead the mind away from these aids. When understanding is reached, these crutches of the imagination can be cast away. Thus Plato uses poetic images as structures that point away from themselves. At the same time he denounces literary productions in which these devices are supposed to have intrinsic value, and are presented as such for imaginative grasp and enjoyment.

The Form of *kalon* has a special role among Forms representing values, for it is the only such Form that has sensibles among its instances (*Phaedrus* 250a, b). The instances are construed by Plato as appearances, and for Plato appearances have a unique dual role. They can mesmerize us, and keep us from going beyond them; or we can see them correctly as mere appearances, requiring explanation in terms of something that transcends them. Hence the special role of beauty; it can chain us to the world of appearances, as physical pleasures do, or it can lead us to the comprehension of other types of fine elements of reality. At its best, the comprehension of beauty leads us away from preoccupation with the senses and with particulars to the understanding of the abstract and the general. Even love is seen by Plato as subordinated to this intellectual Odyssey. What makes Plato's view of love "cold" is not simply the negative attitude toward lust,[4] for that attitude is detachable from the main philosophic claim. Rather, it is the impersonal nature of human bonds. Love and friendship are healthy relationships only as long as they link humans sharing aspirations toward higher goals. Since unconditional loyalty to the individual cannot be justified within this scheme, Plato banishes it from the well-lived life.

V

Plato's Legacy. In conclusion, the thoroughgoing rift between Plato and the Greek culture of his predecessors and contemporaries should be emphasized. His rejection of the *too pathei mathos* principle, and his insistence that aspiration is more important than inspiration, as well as his claim that the articulation of norms for successful living is a matter of rational discoveries analogous to mathematical discoveries—all of these fly in the face of everything that dramatists, statesmen like Pericles, or philosophers before Plato concerning themselves with morality, believed. Some of Aristotle's disagreements with his teacher can be seen as returning to—from the Greek point of view—more traditional ways of thinking.

In rebelling against his cultural heritage, Plato saw clearly the vast difference between abstract theorizing—exemplified for him mostly by the rising science of mathematics—with the general and the abstract as its objects, and living by the consequences of theory on the one hand, and thought in terms of images, stress on the uniqueness of the individual, and thus everyday as well as inspired experience on the other.

He contrasts enlightened rational, practical reasoning not only with the refusal to plan and the pleasure seeking of the vulgar, but also with the inspired, individual-oriented attitudes of art, love, and kindness.

Plato had the insight to see the differences, and the courage to make his choices. Another tradition, Christianity, draws the contrasts in equally stark terms, and draws different conclusions. The two sets of commitments live in an uneasy truce within the modern Western intellectual frameworks.

Right or wrong, both Plato and Christianity have integrated views of human life. Rethinking Plato along the lines suggested in this paper should not only give us a deeper insight into the nature of beauty and art, but should also help us to inquire into the possibility of an integrated view of human life in our own times.

NOTES

1. For a detailed account see J. M. E. Moravcsik, "Reason and Eros in the *Ascent*-Passage of the *Symposium*" in *Essays in Greek Philosophy,* edited by J. P. Anton and G. L. Kustas (Albany: State University of New York Press, 1971), pp. 285–302.

2. The presentation of the claim that Plato's main concern is understanding rather than knowledge can be found in J. M. E. Moravcsik, "Understanding and Knowledge in Plato's Philosophy," *Neue Hefte für Philosophie,* vol. 15/16 (1978), pp. 53–69.

3. This account of Plato's views and the lines of reasoning should be contrasted with such standard accounts as, for example, Rupert C. Lodge, *Plato's Theory of Art* (London: Routledge + Kegan Paul, 1953).

4. This way of interpreting Plato rests on a new interpretation of the charioteer image, introduced in *Phaedrus* 246aff. The conventional modern interpretation for example, R. Hackforth, *Plato's Phaedrus* (Cambridge: Cambridge University Press, 1952) identifies the division of the soul affected in this simile with the division in *Republic* Book 4.

In spite of Plato's own talk of a trichotomy (253c7), this is not what is presented in this passage. Though an adequate defense of the new interpretation is beyond the scope of this chapter, at least a brief outline will be given.

First, there are four ingredients in the simile, not three. There is the charioteer, the two horses, and the wings. Second, the "bad" horse cannot be simply the third part of the soul according to the division of the *Republic*. For while the "bad" horse is described as unqualifiedly bad, not helping in the ascent at all, and not being necessary to the healthy functioning of a human, the third part of the soul in the *Republic* includes the necessary bodily appetites (hunger, thirst) and is never said to be unconditionally bad; in fact, one of the cardinal virtues is associated with its healthy functioning. If we identify the third part of the soul with the "bad" horse of the *Phaedrus* we will have to ascribe to Plato the doctrine of original sin—that is, the view that an essential part of human nature is basically corrupt.

According to the new interpretation, the charioteer image is a combination of the philosophical psychologies of the *Republic* and the *Symposium*. The wings represent the right kind of eros—that is, aspiration. The charioteer is reason (and the accompanying desires, as in *Republic* Book 9, 580d). The "good" horse represents those feelings and desires that can cooperate with reason—thus cutting across the second and third parts of the soul in the division of the *Republic*. The "bad" horse is simply lust.

This does not give an all-inclusive picture of the soul; but neither does the account in *Republic* Book 4. At any given time, Plato singles out only those psychological ingredients that are relevant to the philosophical investigation at hand.

CHAPTER III

Plato on Imitation and Poetry in *Republic* 10

Alexander Nehamas

Plato's attitude toward the poets is bald and uncompromising: He wants no part of them. And though he takes no pleasure in his attitude, for he takes pleasure in poetry, he takes the attitude seriously. His argument in Book 10 of the *Republic* is neither exaggerated nor ironical. He does not rely on two different senses of "imitation" in order to exclude only that part of poetry that it might be thought reasonable to despise. He does not exploit a subtle distinction in order to retain serious poetry once he has succeeded in eliminating poetry that merely entertains. His proscription allows of no exceptions.

But though his view is more stern than it has sometimes been comfortable to suppose, its scope is also narrower. Book 10 of the *Republic* contains an outrageous attack on poetry and—this is part of my argument in what follows—on poetry only. Plato does not "banish the artists." In fact—this is another part of my argument—he does not even banish the painters.[1]

That Plato banishes only poetry, though painting is in his eyes equally *mimesis* (imitation), suggests that being imitative is not by itself a sufficient reason for exclusion from the city. What distinguishes painting from poetry in this respect is a pressing question, especially when we realize (as I hope we shall) that Plato's argument against poetry depends on a series of analogies with painting. These are close enough to have convinced many of Plato's readers, though not Plato himself, that painting and all "fine" art, not only poetry, is to be outlawed. But by turning our attention to the differences between painting and poetry that account for the asymmetry in Plato's treatment of these two practices, we may find that though the action he advocates is, as usual, quite drastic, his motivation, as is also usual, is not half as perverse as we have been fearing.

I

Plato states his position on poetry in the preamble to *Republic* 10 (595a1–c5). This is that "in no way are we admitting [in our city] as much of it as is imitative" (595a5). His reason for holding this position, which he also states in the preamble, is that tragedy and all such imitations

> are hazardous to the reason (dianoia) of their listeners—of those
> at least who do not possess as an antidote the knowledge of what
> these things really are (595b5–7).[2]

We must notice that the subject here is only poetry and that the reason why it is not admitted to the city is that it harms the soul of its listeners. This suggests that Plato is not going on to offer two arguments against poetry—first, that it is imitative (595c7–602b11), and second, that it is bad for the soul (602c1–606d8).[3] Rather, the general discussion of imitation and the demonstration that poetry is one of its species are only parts of the single argument against poetry that we find announced at the very beginning of the book. In addition, noticing this point is helpful in distinguishing Plato's view of poetry from his view of painting, for if being imitative were a reason for banishment, painting, being the paradigm of imitation, should surely be banished. Yet the opening of the book says only that poetry is to be banished. The reason for this, we shall see, is the difference in the seriousness of their bad effects.

Before we turn to this question, however, we must discuss a serious difficulty that the preamble raises for the interpretation of Plato's view of poetry. For though the present claim is that no imitative poetry (hosé mimétiké) is admissible in the city (595a5), the discussion of poetry in Books 2 and 3 concluded by admitting "the unmixed imitator of good character" (ton tou epieikous mimétén akraton 397d4–5). Furthermore, Book 10 itself finally allows "so much of poetry as consists of hymns to the gods and praises of virtuous people" (hoson monon hymnous theois kai

enkómia tois agathois poiéseós, 607a3–4). If such poetry is imitative, Book 10 contradicts not only Book 3 but itself as well. If it is
not, how much poetry is thereby allowed after all in the city?[4]

Plato has been forcefully defended against the charge of incon-
sistency by J. Tate, who, in a series of papers that are still very
influential, argued that Plato uses "imitation" in two senses. The
imitation he banishes at 595a5 is imitation of a bad sort, while the
imitation he admits at 397a4–5 is of a good sort, and the contradiction disappears.[5]

Plato's earlier discussion of imitation in Books 2 and 3 concerns
the elementary education of the young Guardians. In his city, as in
Athens (cf. 376e2–3), children begin their education through poetry. Having discussed the subjects appropriate for them, Plato
goes on (392c6ff) to discuss style (lexis), and distinguishes pure
narration (the dithyramb), pure imitation or impersonation (tragedy),[6] and their combination (epic). He then raises the question
whether the Guardians should be educated by the use of imitation,[7]
and claims that the answer depends on whether they are to be
imitative themselves (394e1–2). It is precisely at this point that Tate
locates the two senses of "imitation"; for, he claims, "the answer
is both 'no' and 'yes.' "[8]

Yet all that Socrates says here is that the young Guardians will be
allowed to imitate only characters like those into which they
should grow (394c4–5). To imitate other sorts as well would be an
instance of polupragmosuné (doing more than one thing; cf.
395b–c) and might make them like the characters they would in that
case imitate. But nothing here, it seems to me, implies that "imitation" has two senses; all that is implied is that one and the same
activity can have different sorts of objects.[9]

Plato now combines the above formal specification of imitation[10]
with the range of its possible subject matter. A good person would
recite mostly by narration, but would occasionally imitate (a) good
people doing good things, (b) less often, good people in bad situations, and (c) only with difficulty and "only for fun" (paidias
charin) bad people doing good things (395c5–e10). An unworthy
person would imitate anything and would use little narration
(397a1–b2). A third style, finally, would consist in a mixture of
these two (397c9–10). Adeimantus now approves only the first of

these three modes, that of "the unmixed imitator of good character" (397d4–5), a sort (I suppose) of a purified Homer.

Tate, however, describes what Adeimantus approves as the

> *nonimitative* style, which nevertheless contains such kinds of imitation as the virtuous poet will not disdain to practice. Plato could scarcely have made it clearer that the style that is nonimitative in the first sense is yet imitative in the second sense, the sense in which the Guardians are imitative.[11]

On Tate's view, therefore, Plato at 595a5 only excludes imitation in the bad sense of 397a1–b2, and nothing else: "The poetry that is admitted is imitative in one sense and nonimitative in another sense."[12]

Plato's attack on poetry is therefore significantly disarmed—if, indeed, it still is an attack at all. But it is clear that *Republic* 394–97 does not generate two senses of "imitation." Plato simply allows the young Guardians to listen to, and to tell, tales that, if they involve imitation, imitate good characters or good actions, and forbids them to do much else. The different styles all imitate in the same sense different objects. The conflict between Books 3 and 10 cannot be resolved in this manner.

In specifying what sorts of poetry are acceptable in Books 2 and 3 of the *Republic,* Plato has consistently enraged generations of readers. We should comment (and we can do no more than that on this occasion) on whether this rage has been justified: Very briefly, my own view is that it has not. Plato's attitude toward what young children should recite, read, and learn from (for *this* is his subject at this point) is quite reasonable. We find it unthinkable that he should imagine that great poetry like Homer's could be harmful. But in thinking of it as "great poetry" we are begging the question, for we place it within a complex cultural context, within a long tradition, and within a world ("Homer's world, not ours," in Auden's words) that we know to be long dead. We do not look at the Homeric poems as a primer, from which one learned to read, to speak, to think, and to value. The relevant comparison is not between ourselves and fourth-century Athenians in respect to our reactions to Homer. (And, in any case, how many *children* today read Homer? And of those who do, in watered-down versions of the *Tales from Homer* type, how many read of Odysseus and

Calypso, or Demodocus' lay of Ares and Aphrodite?)[13] The proper comparison would involve contemporary children, mass education, and mass entertainment. Instead of learning from Homer, children today learn from primers that are often, for example, sexist; we find nothing wrong or narrow-minded in protesting against them. They are entertained by, and learn what friendship and companionship are, from "Starsky and Hutch" and "Donnie and Marie"—ubiquitous and intrusive purveyors of bad taste, deformed paradigms, and questionable values.[14] And though we may not want to legislate such things out of existence, we do not, or would like not to, let children watch them. On the reverse side of this coin, the positive effort that goes into making children's literature appropriate to them, correctly or incorrectly, is a Platonic legacy.

In short, we quite agree with Plato that censorship for children is appropriate. We quite agree with him that art has great power, and that we must channel it correctly. We do not agree on whether censorship should be practiced on Homer (but this, I have argued, depends on a wrong comparison) and on whether it should be legislated by the state. But on the last issue we cannot any longer charge Plato with being a philistine; we can only charge him with being illiberal. And this is neither new, nor surprising, nor (as many have feared about his views on Homer) inconsistent with his own poetic powers.

We still have to face the conflict between Books 3 and 10: The former seems to allow imitative poetry, the latter to forbid it. This conflict, I am afraid, cannot be ultimately eliminated; but it is not as stark and glaring as it has often seemed to be. In discussing this last issue, we shall gain some understanding of why Plato seems to return to the question of poetry in Book 10, something that has made this last part of the *Republic* seem suspiciously like an afterthought.[15] I shall suggest that Plato does not clearly *return* to the banishment of poetry in Book 10, but that he raises the question in a systematic form for the first time. Books 8 and 9 of the *Republic* consist mainly of a discussion of threats against the unity of the soul and of the city. Book 10 belongs primarily with them, and shows that poetry is one of these threats and that the city is proof against it.

Now Book 10 seems to begin with a reference to the earlier

discussion in Book 3, but this reference is not absolutely clear. Socrates does say that he is now convinced (ennoó 595a2) that the city has been well organized (ókizomen; 595a2); his reason for thinking this is that he recalls (enthumétheis, 595a3) that poetry is not being admitted to it (595a5). But I am not certain that we have to take his recollection to refer to the discussion in Book 3, which concerned primarily the control and not the exclusion of poetry. We might instead take it to refer to his realizing that nowhere after Book 3 (to which I shall presently turn) is there any provision made for poetry in the organization of the city: This omission, we should realize, would have been glaring to an Athenian audience, in whose life poetry (tragic, epic, and lyric) played a crucial part. Finally, his comment "It appears even clearer now that it is not to be admitted" (ou paradektea nun kai enargesteron . . . fainetai, 595a5–6) need not be taken to imply that an earlier attempt to banish poetry has already been made, but only that such an attempt, had it been made before the soul had been divided, would have been much more difficult to justify.

The actual discussion of poetry in Books 2 and 3 concerned the elementary education of the young Guardians, and Plato, I think, was quite willing to allow imitative poetry to play a crucial role in that enterprise. He considers the use of poetry proper in education (cf. 376e2–4, where Plato expresses a remarkably positive attitude toward traditional education), since he thinks that imitation can become "habit and nature" (395d1–3);[16] if, therefore, a child's objects of imitation are also examples for imitation, he thinks that they will be beneficial. His claims about poetry (and the other arts, which he does not here contrast with poetry) at 401a–402a show that he is thinking of the very beginning of the Guardians' education.[17] He believes that by proper imitation, a child not yet capable of understanding (prin logon dunatos einai labein, 402a2)[18] can develop a preference for beauty and goodness and will embrace understanding in friendship when it does finally arrive (402a3–4). On this question, Plato anticipates Aristotle, who also thinks that imitation is natural and that human beings "learn at first by imitation,"[19] though Plato differs from Aristotle in thinking that imitation in poetry becomes harmful once understanding has set in— that is, once the soul has developed all its separate parts.[20]

Though children can learn from imitation, the adult inhabitants of the city are not to be exposed to it.[21] This is Plato's primary concern, the main target of his argument in Book 10, and what his refusal to admit poetry in the city comes to; when he writes here that imitative poetry is not being admitted, we need not look for another sense in which imitation is (or has already been) admitted. The discussion in Books 2 and 3 lays the foundations for the omission of any reference to poetry as a component in the city's life in the bulk of the *Republic,* and Book 10 explains why that omission has been made.[22]

Precisely because the foundations for the exclusion of poetry are laid in Books 2 and 3, however, Plato, by the time of his writing of Book 10, has come to see his attitude toward poetry as a single policy. This, at least, is what is suggested by his statement at 607b1–3:

> Let this, then, be said in our defense in recalling that it was reasonable to send poetry away on that occasion since it has such a nature.

For this does refer back to 398a–b, where the poet who imitates everything is not allowed to enter the city. Because of the reference, we cannot totally avoid the conflict between Books 2 and 3 on the one hand and Book 10 on the other, which we have been discussing. But if we realize that there is more to the proscription of poetry than the single passage 398a–b, and that the major burden of that proscription is carried by Plato's silence as to the role of poetry in his city's life, then the conflict loses a great part of its immediacy and seriousness.

Book 10, therefore, can now be seen on a part of the long discussion of the perversions of the soul and of the city that begins with Book 8: Poetry creates a "bad constitution" (kakén politeian, 605b7–8) in the soul just as, for example, an excess or defect of wealth can destroy the "constitution within" the wise man (tén en hautó politeian, 591e1). Though not perfectly consistent with Books 2 and 3, Book 10 is not simply an incomprehensible return to a subject that these two books seem to have exhausted; for a crucial part of its function is to justify the omission of poetry from the life of the city's adult inhabitants—a subject not accounted for in Books 2 and 3. Thus Book 10 of the *Republic* is neither a "digression"[23] nor a "coda,"[24] neither an "appendix"[25] nor a "retrospect."[26] It is, rather, a step of a carefully constructed description of the ways in which the soul can be less than perfect and thus lose the rewards of the life of justice—to a final accounting of which Plato significantly turns in the last part of Book 10.

II

We must now look at the actual argument that Plato offers in Book 10 of the *Republic* for the banishment of poetry—that it brings disarray into the soul. The first part of this argument consists of a discussion of imitation, and the conclusion of that discussion is that imitation is worthless as a source of knowledge and that

> the imitator knows nothing of any accounting about what he imitates and imitation is merely play (paidia) and not anything serious (spoudé). [602b7–8]

But that something is play is not enough to exclude it from the city. This inhuman attitude would be in conflict with Plato's view at 424e5–426a6 that paidia should be forbidden only if it is lawless (paranomos) and thus destroys good character (which is, essentially, Plato's argument against poetry as well). Plato clearly does not dislike paidia for itself,[27] but only if it usurps the place of what must be taken seriously.[28] The demonstration that imitation is merely play does not provide a reason for banishing poetry, but is only one of the steps leading to that final conclusion.

At 595c7 Socrates asks, in his traditional manner, for a definition of imitation;[29] in reaching it, he appeals to the theory of Forms. A number of factors make the appeal strange: First, the theory is not mentioned in the preamble to the book, in contrast to the divided soul, which is;[30] second, the version of the theory that is introduced is enormously peculiar;[31] third, little of what Socrates says about the Forms is actually relevant to his definition of imitation. It is important for him to show that imitation is at two removes from reality. But showing this does not clearly require the dubious one-over-many argument of 596aff, or Forms of artifacts, or God as the creator of such Forms. In addition, the theory here attributes to the craftsman, a knowledge that, being of Forms, has been so far considered as the distinguishing (and very hard to acquire) characteristic of the philosopher. But since these questions are not central to my purpose, I shall not pursue them any farther.[32]

The question that we must ask is why Plato reaches his definition of imitation through a discussion of painting (596d–597a), which he describes as a way of making "things that appear but that are not truly real" (596e4). Since his primary concern is with poetry, why does he not depend directly on its features in order to define imitation?

This is by no means the only occasion where Plato employs this strategy. He introduces painting for the second time in distinguishing the three sorts of objects that there are: natural objects (Forms), physical objects, and painted objects. The painter cannot be said to be a maker of either of the first two, but is only an imitator of what God and the craftsman make.[33] The definition thus reached is this:

> Do you call the imitator [a maker] of the product at two removes from reality?[34] [597e3–4]

Only now is this general definition applied to the tragic poets and all other imitators (597e6–8), who are also said to make things at two removes from "the king" and the truth.[35]

Plato introduces the painter for a third time at 597e10ff and, by means of distinguishing between the way physical objects really are and the way they appear, claims that painting concerns an appearance (fantasma) and not truth—a result that he then generalizes to all imitation (598b6–8).[36] Again, he argues that the painter's products are deceitful, and that therefore this is true of all imitation.[37] After a detailed discussion of poetry on the basis of these conclusions, the painter is used to introduce the additional argument for the imitator's ignorance (601b9–602b8). Finally, the appeal of imitation to the lower parts of the soul is also introduced by means of painting, and only then is it generalized to poetry (602cff).

But why does Plato depend so crucially on painting? We tend quite automatically to take painting as our model for the representational arts, and this procedure has raised few questions.[38] But the little we know about the early history of mimeisthai ("to imitate") and its cognates suggests that these terms were originally connected with speech and poetry rather than with painting, with hearing rather than with seeing. In view of this, Plato's practice of depending on painting for his views of imitation and poetry needs to be explained.

In an important though idiosyncratic work, Hermann Koller has argued that *mimesis* was originally connected with music and dancing and that its sense was therefore that of "representation" and even "expression" rather than of "imitation."[39] He finds this last sense, which he claims is specific to painting, invented in *Republic* 10.[40] Some of Koller's conclusions have been criticized by Gerald Else,[41] but one serious aspect of the problem seems to me not to have been completely resolved.

In disagreeing with Koller, Else tries to find in the earliest occurrences of these terms the connotation of counterfeiting and its attendant distinction between appearing and being, which he considers crucial to the sense "imitation." But this effort, it seems to me, fails. Consider, for example, the *Delian Hymn to Apollo,* where (163) it is said that the Delian maidens

> know how to *imitate* the voice and dance of all people. (pantón d' anthrópón fónas kai krembaliastun mimeisth' isasin)

Koller, because of the presence of dancing, thinks that the sense of "imitation" is totally inappropriate here;[42] Else, by contrast, finds it unavoidable.[43] But when we think of the continuation, "anyone would think that he himself was speaking, so well is their song put together," it seems to me that though the connection with music proves little, we need not suppose that the maidens "impress and flatter their guests by imitating their native accents and dances" either.[44] Rather, the maidens are said actually to speak different dialects and to know how to perform dances from difference areas: They *act like* other people, and no deception is involved.

The case is quite similar with Aeschylus, *Choephoroi* 564:

> amfó de fónén ésomen parnésida glóssés autén Fókidos mimoumenó

Else's translation, "we will put forward a Parnassian accent, imitating [mimicking] the sound of the Phocian dialect," seems to me gratuitous.[45] Orestes may much more plausibly be taken to be telling Pylades, who was Phocian to begin with, that they must, quite simply, speak Phocian to each other.

The sense of *acting like* someone else is, we should notice, exactly what is needed in interpreting Theognis 370:

> mómeuntai de moi polloi . . . mimeisthai d' oudeis tón asotón dunatai.

To account for this case, Else needs to postulate a second sense of the verb, "an extension of the meaning from physical mimicry to moral imitation."[46] But on my suggestion the line can be smoothly translated as

> Many make fun of me . . . but none of the unwise can act like me.[47]

It does not, therefore, seem clear that *mimesis* was from its very beginning connected with *mimicking*. It is clear that the term and its cognates were more often used in connection with speaking and acting rather than with painting, and it is also clear that even in the latter half of the fifth century they did not go hand in hand with the Platonic notions of the counterfeit, the merely apparent, the deceitful, and the fake.[48] A number of cases in Herodotus illustrate very well the sense *acting like* that we have found above.[49] Thucydides' claim that Pausanias' behavior "appeared more like a *mimesis* of tyranny than like a generalship" and that cost him his life could not be explained by appealing to the sense *counterfeiting*; on the contrary, the necessary sense seems to be that of *emulating*.[50] Even Democritus, who did in fact rely on the distinction between seeming and being in many aspects of his thinking, does not seem to me to appeal to it, as Else claims he does,[51] in DK B39:

> One must either be or imitate a good human being. (agathon é einai chreòn é mimeisthai)

It is not plausible to take this as advice to pretend to be good. Rather, we should take it as advice to the effect that, if one cannot be good, one should do the next best thing—act like someone who is.[52]

By the end of the fifth century, however, the contrast between imitation and reality may be found in the dramatic poets—for example, Aristophanes *Frogs* 108–9 and Euripides *Ion* 1429.[53] It seems to me plausible that this connection might have been already established in painting, especially if we consider Xenophon *Mem.* III.x.1–8 as an accurate report. In that passage, the "illusionist" painter Parrhasius eagerly agrees with Socrates that painting is a "likeness of the visible" (eikasia tón horómenón, x.1) and insists that all that he can imitate (apomimeisthai, miméton) is the look, and not the character, of people. Parrhasius is finally persuaded, however, that character can also be imitated—but only insofar as it "appears through (diafainei) the face and bearing" of the subject. A similar connection between painting and appearance is made in Socrates' ensuing conversation with the sculptor Cleiton. Even though Xenophon's evidence is hardly contemporary (Parrhasius seems to have been born before 460 B.C.[54] and this conversation may have occurred around 420–410), the report does give some evidence that a connection between painting and the way things look may have been in existence by the end of the fifth century.

We are now in a position to explain why Plato relies so heavily on painting in his discussion of imitation in *Republic* 10.[55] "Imitation," as it was traditionally applied to poetry, speaking, and dancing, meant primarily *acting like* someone else. It did not carry with it the connotation of imitating only the appearance as opposed to the reality of the object imitated, or the connected notion of deceiving and counterfeiting. In fact, the crucial role that poetry played in education seems to have depended precisely on a conflation between appearance and reality.[56] Plato, however, wants to argue in *Republic* 10 that the poets, even when their imitations are successful, can do no more than imitate the look, not the nature, of things. To make this controversial point, to argue that poetry really is not just imitation in the sense of *likeness* but imitation of *appearance*, Plato appeals to painting, which can easily be said to be an imitation of the look of its subjects, considers it as representative of all imitation, and applies its characteristics to poetry as well.

It has long been claimed both by opponents and by defenders of Plato's views on art that artists need not imitate only sensible objects (which they do, according to Plato, by reproducing their appearance) but also that they can somehow directly imitate the Forms. This idea, whose later origin (notably in Plotinus)[57] has been noticed by M. H. Abrams and Monroe Beardsley,[58] has been connected in various ways with Plato. Some claim merely that it is compatible with his view of art as imitation,[59] while others argue more strongly that Plato actually believed that art imitates the Forms.[60]

Both versions of this approach to Plato are wrong, textually and philosophically. The main texts on which it is based are either neutral on this question or they contradict this very claim they are used to support. For example, Tate appeals to *Republic* 402b–c in order to show that "the truly mousikos (musical) perceives the ideas and their images."[61] Now, it is true that this passage mentions forms (eidé) of virtues. But these forms are not the Forms of Plato's theory, which have not yet been introduced at this point of the *Republic*. The presence of the word ειδο is clearly not sufficient to establish the presence of the theory, especially since these forms are present in sensible objects (enonta) and not separate from them, as the theory requires them to be. The passage only claims that we must learn to recognize the many varieties of virtues and vices in the world and in our images of them. The implication, in Adam's words, is that the poet "copies from the life" and not from the intelligible world.[62]

Republic 500e–501b, a passage often used in this connection, likens the construction of the perfect city to the work of a painter using "a divine paradigm" (501e3). Tate considers this as a description of the "genuine kind of imitation."[63] But this misses the point of Plato's simile, which is not that there is such a painter, but that this is what the philosopher is. Nor is *Republic* 472d helpful in locating a painter who imitates the Forms,[64] for though the passage shows that Plato did not think that artists are confined to reproducing the appearance only of actually existing things, this does not imply that in painting someone more beautiful than any existing person, the painter would be imitating the Form.[65]

We close this discussion with two texts outside the *Republic*. First, *Laws* 817b–c, which claims that the inhabitants of Plato's city are the true tragedians, for they live the best life—the truest tragedy. Far from supporting the claim that true poetry imitates the Forms,[66] this passage makes the same point as *Republic* 500e–501b: The best kind of poetry is not poetry at all, but a good life; hence, unless by virtue of a pun, there is no good poetry.[67] Second, *Phaedrus* 248d–e, a much misread passage in which the "musical" (mousikos) is among the best kinds of life that a soul can choose, in contrast to the life of the imitator, which is sixth down Plato's list. Taking "musical" to refer to some sort of artist, commentators have seen Plato here distinguishing between a true artist and a mere imitator.[68] But the *Phaedrus* has been discussing the soul and the proper relations between its parts. The best lives are lived by the most harmonious souls. And for such souls we find the term mousikótatos ("most musical," *Republic* 411e–412a; cf. mousikos 591d1). This is the person who uses musical and physical education for their true purpose, the harmonious agreement of reason and spirit which produces control over appetite. This, and not "the arranger of strings," is the true musician—the liberal, civilized character whom Plato considers responsible for one of the best sorts of life a human being can have.[69] The "musical", in this as well as in other contexts, is not the artist but the gentleman who patronizes the artists and knows what to take from them.[70]

Turning to the philosophical basis of the idea that art can imitate the Forms, we should begin by recalling the persistent commonplace that in *Republic* 10 Plato accuses art of being an imitation of an imitation. But in fact Plato never says this, either in this book or in any other part of his work. Further, not once in *Republic* 10 is *mimesis* used to refer to the relationship between sensible objects and Forms.[71]

Plato does say, once, that the craftsman makes things "looking toward" (pros . . . blepón 596b7) the Form, but this is not sufficient to establish that the relationship between the product and the Form is one of imitation[72]—that is, nothing in the text implies that the relationship between a work of art and its subject is the same as that between a physical object and its Form or Forms.[73] And this is one of the main philosophical reasons why the painter and the poet cannot imitate the Forms, for this would just be to produce physical objects—beds or good people. To "imitate" the Forms is a request that it is logically impossible for the artist to satisfy,[74] for in virtue of satisfying it, the artist would cease to be an artist.

In his remarks on this subject, Collingwood wrote that the artist "makes not a bed or a battle or a hero or a villain, but an object *sui generis,* to be judged not by the standards by which such things are judged, but by a standard peculiar to itself."[75] Collingwood, indeed, tried to show that Plato thought of art as an activity distinct from all others: not knowledge, not perception, but imagination— with its own laws, principles, and values, and even with its own way to truth. Though not unlike Collingwood's own philosophy, this is exactly the reverse of Plato's view of art, for there is little that is more striking in Plato's attitude than his absolute refusal to accord to the activity and to the products of *mimesis* an independent status of their own.

This refusal is presupposed, for example, by his crucial statement at *Republic* 394e8–9 that

> the same person is not capable of imitating many things well as he can one,

a statement that is an application of the principle that each person can be good only at one practice. Here the conditions for what constitutes a distinct activity are not supplied by the activity itself, not by the rules it follows, but only by its object: if the object is different, the imitation is different too.[76] Playing the hero, Plato seems to think, is an activity distinct from playing the villain (395b3–6); it is his commitment to such a position that underlies his unwillingness to allow the poet who can imitate anything and everything (398a–b) into his city. And despite his one later reference to *mimesis* as an object of knowledge, it is remarkable how little Plato thinks of it as an art along with the many other arts that he discusses in the *Republic* (cf. 601a4–6).

When one turns from the practice of *mimesis* to its objects, the picture remains the same. The objects of imitations are hardly entities in their own right. Even to speak of "an appearance of a bed" is slightly misleading in this context, for appearances can be thought to have their own ontological status. But Plato seems to block this approach by insisting that the painter produces *a bed*; and though it is a bed "in a way" (tropó ge tini 596e10) this seems to qualify more the degree than the manner in which the imitator's product is a bed.[77] Thus Plato speaks of a painter making not a picture of a cobbler, but "a cobbler who seems to be"

(600e7–601a7). Imitation, he says, can "fashion *everything*, because it touches everything in small part—and that is an image" (598b6–8).

Plato's metaphysical view is manifested in a linguistic vacillation on his part. At 598b4–5 he characterizes painting as an "*imitation* of appearance" and not of reality (fantasmatos mimésis), while at 599a2–3 he claims that poets "*produce* appearances" (fantasmata poiousin). Similarly, he characterizes poets as "*imitators* of images" at 600e5. (mimétas eidólon), while he describes Homer as a "*maker* of an image" at 599d3 (eidolou démiourgos). To think of an artist as an imitator of appearance is to think of the appearance as the *object* of imitation, as something existing in the world before the artist begins to work, as what the artist copies or represents. The appearance in this case is a part of the physical object that is the artist's model. To think of an artist as a maker of an appearance, by contrast, is to think of the appearance as the *product* of imitation, as something that comes into being as a result of the artist's work, as the result of the artist's representation. That Plato does not seem to mark this distinction has some important implications, since it suggests that he is thinking of the object of imitation and of the product of imitation as being the same object— if not in number, at least in type. It almost seems as if he believes that the painter lifts the surface off the subject and transplants it onto the painting; this idea is also suggested, we should notice, by his use of the word efaptesthai at 598b7–8, which we quoted above: Imitation, he claims, *touches* a small part of everything—the image. This image is both the surface of the subject and the product of the painter; the difference between the painted bed and the real bed is that, though they have identical appearances, the latter is in three dimensions while the former is only an image with no depth.

On such a view the limiting case of imitation is the creation of a duplicate of the model. This metaphysical version of the story of Pygmalion is not only consistent with Plato's attitude, but also actually occurs in the famous passage 432a–c of the *Cratylus,* for Socrates argues there that if one took an image (eikón) of Cratylus and proceeded to add to the color and shape already belonging to it (the appearance) everything else that belongs to Cratylus, then the final product will be a second Cratylus. Thus the painted Cratylus is conceived as an incomplete Cratylus, as the very appearance, which is only part of the real Cratylus, and which can be turned into the latter simply by the addition of details that it lacks.

Thus the imitator of an F thing produces a seeming F thing, an object whose identity is constituted by the thing that it seems to be, not by any properties that it might have in its own right. And that its objects lack such properties is a central reason why *mimesis* is in Plato's eyes not an art; for it would have to be such properties, and only such properties, that could provide criteria for when the practice was and when it was not pursued well and an account of what the practice consists in.[78] As it is, if we try to base such criteria on the objects imitated rather than on their imitations themselves, then the result simply is that a painting of, say, a bed is better the more what it produces looks like a real bed, and the more practice itself looks like carpentry. My suspicion is that this is precisely what Plato thinks, and that it is the reason why he does not accord imitation an independent status of its own.[79]

Plato's view in the *Republic* is, I think, inconsistent with his statement in the *Sophist* that "an image, though not really being [what it is an image of], really is [an image]" (240b12–13). But to come to that conclusion Plato had to revise substantially a number of views he held when he wrote the *Republic*, and we cannot discuss these issues on this occasion. Our present concern is with what we might call the utter transparency of imitation, its almost total lack of substantiality both as practice and as product. It is precisely this transparency that, in Plato's eyes, justifies one of his most extreme views, that

> if one could make both things, both what is imitated and the image, do you think that anyone would abandon himself to the making of images and consider that as his most precious possession in life?[80] [599a6–b1; cf. 599b3–7]

As the products of *mimesis* are images of real things, so the practice of *mimesis* is the image of a real practice. The point of the first part of the argument against poetry in Book 10 of the *Republic* is to demonstrate the total heteronomy of *mimesis*. Being thus heteronomous, the imitation of the waging of war, the governing of cities, and the improvement of character can proceed without even true opinion (pistis) about such issues, much less knowledge (epistēmē) about them.[81]

III

Everything that has been said so far, however, makes *mimesis* "some sort of game and nothing serious" (paidian tina kai ou spoudén, 602b8), and though this is indeed a lowly status, it does not justify its banishment. It is only after this part of his argument has been completed, at 602c1ff, that Plato goes on to show, by means of the divided soul, why poetry (which now more clearly becomes the subject of his discussion) is to be excluded from the city.

Plato's argument for this conclusion is immensely complicated, and not always very clear.[82] Its first stage depends, as we have said, on yet another analogy (the last) between painting and poetry. Plato writes that painting "exploits a weakness in our nature" (hémón tó pathémati tés fuseós epithemené)—namely, our susceptibility to error and illusion (602c7–d5). By contrast, measuring, counting, and weighing help us in "being ruled" not by what appears to be the case but by the results of calculation (602d6–9). Calculation is attributed to the logistikon en té psyché (602e1–2), the calculating part of the soul, which was distinguished from spirit and appetite at 436ff. Sometimes, it seems, though the calculating part has performed its measurements, contrary results still appear to it (tanantia fainetai 602e4–6).[83] Yet "we have agreed that it is impossible for the same thing to have contrary opinions about the same matters" (602e8–9). As Murphy points out,[84] this is not, strictly speaking, accurate, since it is not clear that the principle stated and discussed at 436a–437d can cover contrary opinions. Still, how the division is accomplished is less important to our purposes than its results.

For what is it that this logically imperfect principle divides? And into what does it divide it? I find the obvious answer, that the soul is divided into reason and appetite once again, difficult to accept. For one thing, this would involve the attribution of thinking to appetite.[85] And though this is not a serious difficulty, the suggestion raises the more difficult question of what the appetite has to do with perceptual error and illusion. Why should our *desire* tell us that the immersed stick is bent?

Most importantly, however, the idea that the soul is here divided into reason and appetite would entail that the principle on which the division depends has been wrongly applied. At 439a–b, for example, the principle was used to show that if the soul has two opposed tendencies, then the soul itself has two parts, not that there is another object, distinct from the soul, that is the subject of one of the opposing tendencies. The principle claims that if an object O has two opposed tendencies T^1 and T^2, then O consists of two parts, O^1 and O^2, each one of which bears one of the two tendencies; not that O bears one tendency and a distinct object, P, the other. Since in our present passage the calculating part of the soul is said to have two opposing beliefs (602e4–6), it must be the calculating part itself that is further divided. Our principle does not allow us to introduce a distinct object, appetite, and attribute to it one of the two conflicting beliefs.

If this is so, we can take Plato to be distinguishing between two aspects of reasoning, both belonging to the rational part of the soul: the uncritical acceptance of the senses' reports on the one hand, and reflective judgments about them on the other. This may seem more plausible if we look at Plato's anatomy of the soul as an attempt to characterize different and partially independent sources of human motivation.[86] His original division of the soul in Book 4 distinguished, very roughly, among rational, emotional, and appetitive motives. His present argument is making a finer distinction within our rational motives. In fact, Plato seems to be appropriating Socrates' account of the only two possible sources of motivation in the *Protagoras* (356c–357a). Socrates had argued there that human action was motivated either by "the power of appearance" (hé tou fainomenou dunamis) or by "the measuring art" (hé metriké techné), and that if the latter were present, it would always dominate. In this passage, Plato seems to be arguing that these are by no means the only sources of motivation, since they are species of rational motivation only, and that Socrates' model in the *Protagoras* was overly simple. More importantly, he also seems to be arguing that the measuring art is not always victorious over the power of appearance. Sometimes we act on

what our senses tell us, sometimes on what we know to be the case
despite what they tell us, and sometimes on what they tell us
despite our knowledge that it is not the case.

The only consideration that might make us think again before
considering that what is opposed to measurement is a part of the
rational part of the soul is the contempt with which Plato seems to
speak of it at 603a7–b4, especially his use of the derogatory term
faulon ("base") at 603a7 and b4. However, in an extremely similar
context in the *Philebus* we read the following:

> . . . if one were to set apart from each art arithmetic, and
> measuring and weighing, might we say that the remaining part of
> each would be base (faulon)?
> It would indeed be base (faulon). [55e1–4]

The part that is left of each art is that part that depends on
experience and trial and error. The fact that Plato is willing to
consider such lower-level cognitive activities as "base" shows
that he may well be using that term in our present passage to
describe a lowly aspect of the soul's rational element.[87]

Having made this distinction, Plato goes on to discuss poetry in
detail (603b6ff). And it is clear that in what follows his argument
against poetry depends on his view that it appeals to and
strengthens the irrational elements in the soul. For example, it is
difficult to interpret differently his discussion of giving in to grief
and tears at 603e–604a (cf. 606a) and his putting together reason
and custom (logos kai nomos), enjoining one to be controlled on
the one hand, and the passion itself (auto to pathos) pulling one
toward grieving on the other at 604a–b. This is surprising because
the discussion of painting seemed to have little if anything to do
with the irrational elements of the soul. Still, I think that this
incongruity is only apparent and that neither Plato nor my account
is incoherent.

The difference is that in his discussion of painting Plato has been
concerned only with the effect of painting, whatever its subject
matter, on its spectator. His claim has been that at least sometimes
painting induces us to think of a painted object as real, and even to
persist in thinking so despite our knowledge that it is not (602d1–4;
cf. 598c1–4). But the first part of his discussion of poetry

(602b6–605a7) is concerned not with the effect of poetry on its audience, but with the subject matter of the poem itself. This is shown by the fact that the discussion opens with a careful statement of what poems are about at 603cd–8; poems, Plato writes, represent people acting willingly or unwillingly, thinking themselves to profit or to be harmed by their actions, and in all such situations (en toutois dé pasin) either grieving or rejoicing. And in all such situations (en hapasi toutois) no agent is in harmony with himself: Everyone is torn by conflict (603c10–d7). This conflict, we have seen, concerns reason and what is irrational in the soul; but it is, as the passage makes clear, part of the subject matter of poetry. Plato claims that poetry represents such conflict becuase it must in most cases depict behavior springing from irrational motives (604e1–6); the poets, if they are to be successful among the many, must depict the "irascible and variable" character (605a2–6). Poetry, therefore, tends to appeal to the irrational aspect of the soul much more than painting, since the domination of reason is what gives most poets their object of imitation. Moreover, in this passage Plato seems to oppose reason both to spirit (thumos) and to appetite (epithumétikon). It has been claimed that this is evidence that he was never serious about the existence of spirit or emotion as a part of the soul in the first place.[88] But emotion is in fact a source of motivation, and Plato thought so for good reasons.[89] The explanation of why he opposes reason to spirit and appetite together, it seems to me, is simply that he does not need to distinguish these two for his present purposes. He wants to claim that poetry is likely to depict conflicts between reason on the one hand and some lower part of the soul on the other. Sometimes, that lower part is appetite (for example, afrodisia, epithumétika, 601d1–2); sometimes it is spirit (for example, achthos, lupé 603e7–8; thumos, 606d1). And this is why he describes what the poets depict by using the terms "irascible and variable" (605a5), which have been associated, respectively, with spirit and appetite in his earlier discussion.[90]

Now, finally, poetry is banished (605a–c). And Plato's reason for this is that he thinks that poetry is much more dangerous to the soul than painting. Poetry's threat is in two parts. Both practices are imitative, and thus both imitate (or produce) deceptive appearances, appearances that we tend to take as reality even in the knowledge that they are not so. This claim, which was made for painting at 602c1–603b5, is made explicitly for poetry at 605b8–c4. To this extent painting and poetry are analogous.

But the appearance that poetry presents as reality is not only much more compelling (because of the greater complexity of poetry, especially dramatic poetry, as an art form), but also, in Plato's eyes, irrational and bestial as well. Even if poetry depicted virtuous characters, it would do no more than to create a way in which someone who *seemed* virtuous, but who might in no way *be* virtuous, would act. To consider that as what constitutes virtue (to take that appearance as reality, an attitude common enough to be natural) would have been repellent enough to him:

> *Prosōpon,* the Greek word for mask, also means face, aspect, person, and stage figure (*persona*); we should allow mask and face to draw semantically close together, and then we should enrich the face far beyond our own conception, until it is able to embrace (as it did for the Greeks from the time of Homer) *the look of a man together with the truth about* him.[91]

This attitude toward the mask, or the appearance in general, is exactly what horrifies Plato, for it occurred not only in what he took to be the best of cases, those where an apparently good character is presented as really good, but much more dangerously, it also occurred in the more common cases where what Plato would consider vicious characters were presented by the poets as good. This is worse than simply to confuse the metaphysics of one's audience—though, to be sure, the theater always does this.[92] It is to pervert one's audience in such a way that they would no longer be able (as Plato thought the Athenians were not) to tell the good from the bad, or to act on the good even if they knew what it was.

Plato's argument against poetry thus involves, first, the opposition of reason to the irrational parts of the soul, which is involved in the subject matter of poetry and in what aspects of the personality it influences (cf. 606d1–7); second, it involves the opposition between two aspects of reasoning, which is involved in explaining why one can be tempted to act even on what one knows not to be correct. It is this opposition that accounts for our tendency to take as models for imitation what are merely products of imitation.

Painting, whatever it depicts, is trivial compared to poetry (cf.598b8–c4); painting is truly a paidia and no more. But poetry can be of harm even to the best among us: This is the gravest (megiston) objection against it (605c6–8, c10, 606b5–8). The best people must be those who can, at least in principle, distinguish between representation and reality, those who know the distance between the theater and life and that one is not to behave in the world as characters are made to behave in poetry (605d–e). But even such people, Plato insists, finally succumb: They, too, take pleasure (chairomen, 605d3) and praise the poet who can make them act in the theater as they would be ashamed to act in life,[93] and who finally succeeds in making them act that way in life as well.

Despite the pleasure he obviously took in poetry himself,[94] Plato was willing to banish it because he saw it only as an imitation of an education, and of a bad education at that. What he allows of poetry at 607a4, "hymns to the gods and praises of noble people," seems to me negligible and tailor-made for special occasions.[95] The question he does not seem to have asked (or perhaps he did, and his theory of the soul gave him the wrong answer)[96] was why even the best people do take pleasure in poetry, why they rejoice in characters distressed, sorrowful, and suffering, why they enjoy being involved in awful, horrible disasters—why, that is, the phenomenon called "distance" today occurs. Had he asked that question, he might have noticed two things. First, that what is at fault for our taking representation for reality may not be the deceitful nature of representation itself, but our own wrong views about it—for example, the assumption that to represent the world is to duplicate its surface, which implies that a representation is a sort of partial object, that an appearance is an incomplete reality. To question this assumption is to take the first step toward granting representation a status of its own. And in taking this step, he might also have noticed that the pleasure of the best people is not at the sorrow represented but at the representation of the sorrow. He might have seen what he did not, that poetry and representation, imitation in general, can be done badly or that it can be done well, that it is, in a word, art.

NOTES

1. I would like to express my gratitude to Professors J. M. E. Moravcsik and Philip Temko, who organized the conference on Plato's philosophy of art and beauty for which this chapter was written. An early version was delivered at Princeton University in February 1979. John Cooper's exhaustive remarks on the text of that version were invaluable, and I hope that the improvements they occasioned have met some of his original misgivings. James Bogen, Charles Young, and Cass Weller were kind enough to discuss aspects of the paper with me. The financial support of the National Endowment of the Humanities is also gratefully acknowledged.

2. Cf. 598d4–5, 605c5–8, 606b5–7. The term akouontes ("listeners") given Plato's contrast between akoé (hearing) and opsis (sight), which pertains to painting (603b6–7), suggests that Plato is avoiding (not forgetting) to mention the painter on this occasion.

3. Cf. James Adam, *The Republic of Plato* (Cambridge: Cambridge University Press, 1921), vol. II, p. 408, n. on 603b–605c: "Poetry, is . . . the counterpart of Painting; its products are low in point of truth, and it feeds our lower nature. We exclude the Poet from our city on both grounds." This view of the structure of Plato's argument is shared, with greater or lesser clarity, by Alistair Cameron, *Plato's Affair with Tragedy* (Cincinnati: O.: University of Cincinnati Press, 1978), p. 47; E. F. Carritt, *The Theory of Beauty* (London: Methuen, n.d.), p. 39; R. C. Cross and A. D. Woozley, *Plato's Republic: A Philosophical Commentary* (New York: St. Martin's Press, 1966), p. 275; William Chase Greene, "Plato's View of Poetry," *Harvard Studies in Classical Philology,* 29 (1918), pp. 1–75, esp. pp. 52–53; G. M. A. Grube, *Plato's Thought* (New York: Oxford University Press, 1964), pp. 189–92; Eva Keuls, "Plato on Painting," *American Journal of Philology,* 95 (1974), pp. 100–27, esp. p. 100; Leonard Moss, "Plato and the *Poetics,*" *Philological Quarterly,* 50 (1971), pp. 533–42, esp. pp. 536–37; Richard Lewis Nettleship, *Lectures on the Republic of Plato* (New York: St. Martin's Press, 1968), pp. 341–43; Eva Schaper, *Prelude to Aesthetics* (London: Allen and Unwin, 1968), pp. 44–47; Paul Shorey, *The Republic of Plato* (London: Heinemann, 1935), vol. II, p. lxii; Shorey, *What Plato Said,* abr. ed. (Chicago, Ill.: University of Chicago Press, 1965), p. 201. I. M. Crombie, *An Examination of Plato's Doctrines* (London: Routledge & Kegan Paul, 1962), vol. I, p. 145, notices that the imitativeness of poetry does not by itself constitute an argument against it in Plato's eyes, but does not develop the point.

4. For example, Paul Friedländer, *Plato: An Introduction* (Princeton, N.J.: Princeton University Press, 1969), vol. I, pp. 122–23, claims that all of Plato's dialogues (which he considers as poetry) are thus allowed back into the city. Cf. Morriss Henry Partee, "Plato's Banishment of Poetry," *Journal of Aesthetics and Art Criticism,* 29 (1970), pp. 209–22, esp. p. 219. R. G. Collingwood, *The Principles of Art* (Oxford: Clarendon Press, 1938), p. 48, argues that Plato does not want to exclude Pindar or lyric poetry in general.

5. J. Tate, " 'Imitation' in Plato's *Republic,*" *Classical Quarterly,* 22 (1928), pp. 16–23; "Plato and 'Imitation,' " *Classical Quarterly,* 26 (1932), pp. 161–69; "Plato, Art, and Mr. Maritain," *The New Scholasticism,* 12 (1938), pp. 107–42. Tate's resolution of the conflict is accepted by, among others, Cross and Woczley, *Plato's Republic,* p. 279; W. J. Verdenius, *Mimesis:* Plato's *Doctrine of Artistic Imitation and Its Meaning to Us* (Leiden: Brill, 1949), pp. 21–24; Whitney J. Oates, *Plato's View of Art* (New York: Charles Scribner's Sons, 1972), p. 36. A variant of Tate's

view is held by all those who think that according to Plato good art imitates the Forms; on this position see n. 60 below. Grube, *Plato's Thought*, p. 186 n. 3, notes his disagreement with Tate, but does not attempt to resolve the difficulty. Shorey, *The* Republic *of Plato*, vol. II, p. 419 n. *c*, makes use of a similar distinction.

6. Cf. Grube, *Plato's Thought*, pp. 185–86. Plato here characterizes imitation as "making oneself like another either in voice or in bearing" (393c5–6).

7. Some find at 394a7–9 an anticipation of the argument of Book 10; cf. Shorey, *The* Republic *of Plato*, vol. I, p. 232. Adam, *The* Republic *of Plato*, vol. I, p. 147, n. on 394d and vol. II, p. 384, n. on 595a, doubts that such a connection is made here. For reasons that will appear below, I accept Adam's view.

8. Tate, " 'Imitation' in Plato's *Republic*," p. 17.

9. Tate seems to me actually to concede this point when he writes that the two "sorts" of imitation are "formally" the same thought "really" very different (" 'Imitation' in Plato's *Republic*," pp. 17–18). The only real difference is in the objects imitated, and this is not sufficient to generate two different kinds of imitation.

10. Plato's distinctions between different forms of recitation, also found in Aristotle's *Poetics*, 1448a20–22, are repeated without significant alteration by René Wellek and Austin Warren, *Theory of Literature* (New York: Harcourt, Brace & World, 1942), pp. 215–16.

11. Tate, " 'Imitation' in Plato's *Republic*," p. 18, my italics.

12. Tate, "Plato on 'Imitation,' " p. 161.

13. On difficulties with sexually explicit passages in Homer, cf. W. E. Gladstone, *Studies on Homer and the Homeric Age* (Oxford: Oxford University Press, 1858), vol. II, pp. 238–64.

14. "Art delights in unsavoury trivia and in the endless proliferation of senseless images (television)," in Iris Murdoch, *The Fire and the Sun: Why Plato Banished the Artists* (Oxford: Oxford University Press, 1977), p. 65.

15. So, recently, Gerald F. Else, *The Structure and Date of Book 10 of Plato's* Republic (Heidelberg, 1972), followed now by Laszlo Versenyi, "Plato and Poetry: The Academician's Dilemma," in John H. D'Arms and John W. Eadie, *Ancient and Modern: Essays in Honor of Gerald Else* (Ann Arbor: University of Michigan Press, 1977), pp. 119–38.

16. The porró ("for long") of 395d1 should not be taken to imply that Plato thinks that the Guardians will engage in imitation for many years. This passage is actually concerned with the dangers of imitating bad models, and the word qualifies the situation of someone who is a good person to begin with: Even such a person, if allowed to imitate bad models for a long time, may become bad. With 395c7–d1, hina mé ek tés miméseós tou einai apolausósin, cp. *Prot.* 326a3–4, hina ho pais zélón mimétai kai oregétai toioutos genesthai.

17. Cf. *Rep:* 376e–377b, which puts training in poetry and music before training in physical education. This is the earliest education given to children. The same point is made at *Prot.* 325a–326b, which describes learning the alphabet, poetry, and the playing of the cithara as the first education outside the home; only later is physical education introduced as an activity to be pursued by children (326b6ff). Cf. also *Laws* 654a6–7, thómen paideian eirai prótén dia Mousón te kai Apollónos . . ., ("Shall we consider that the earliest education is that which proceeds through the Muses and Apollo?"). Isocrates, *Antidosis* 266–68, characterizes the education of young children (hén hoi paides en tois didaskaleiois poiountai) as education concerning letters and music; *Antidosis* 183 places practice in gymnastics along with training in philosophy, and this considerably later in life.

18. According to one tradition in Stoicism, probably deriving from Zeno, reason comes into human beings at the age of fourteen; according to another, reported by Aëtius, and probably due to Chrysippus, the age of which reason is developed is the próté hebdomas—that is, the seventh year of life. Cf. Hans von Arnim, *Stoicorum Veterum Fragmenta* (Leipzig: Teubner, 1905–24), vol. I, pp. 40–41.

19. *Poetics* 1448b5–9. Moss, "Plato and the *Poetics*," p. 540, thinks that, in contrast to Aristotle, Plato considers imitation to be an "acquired taste." But both our present passage and 607e, to which he also refers, support the contrary conclusion. Cf. *Rep.* 595a–b; Plato's statement that poetry harms its listeners' *reason* and that the discussion of its banishment had to wait for the division of the soul suggests that adult and underage audiences may react differently to poetry.

20. It is characteristic of Plato to consider a necessary step in an upward progression as something to be discarded and even despised once it has performed its function. This is clear, for example, in the ascent of *eros* in the *Symposium:* The beauty of a single body does not only cease to be an object of love once the lover has been enabled, partly by its means, to perceive the beauty of all bodies; it actually becomes an object of contempt (katafronésanta). Plato expresses a similar attitude in connection with an epistemic ascent at *Rep.* 516a–b.

21. Plato does not seem to envisage the composition of new poems once a sufficient repertory has been established; cf. 424b3–c6, where he fears that new poems may introduce surreptitiously unacceptable new modes of composition and recitation.

22. The only other mention of poetry in such a context outside Book 10 is at 586b, where tragedians are excluded from the city, quite incidentally, "because they praise tyranny."

23. Nettleship, *Lectures on the* Republic *of Plato*, p. 340.

24. Crombie, *An Examination of Plato's Doctrines*, vol. I, p. 143.

25. Shorey, *The* Republic *of Plato*, vol. II, p. lxi.

26. Adam, *The* Republic *of Plato*, vol. II, p. 384, n. on 595a–597e.

27. At *Laws* 685a6–b1 Plato characterizes the whole enterprise of that work as a paidia of old men; and at 803c2–8 he describes people as playthings (paignia) of the gods, and living as play (paizonta . . . paidias . . . diabiónai). *Tim.* 52d2 describes physical science as paidia.

28. See the discussion of how philosophy must not be pursued as a game at *Rep.* 539c5–d1; and cp. *Soph.* 237b10–c4.

29. mimésin holós echois an moi eipein hoti pot' estin; This question, and the ensuing discussion with Glaucon on the difficulty of the problem, suggest that little of theoretical importance for imitation was established in Books 2 and 3.

30. This may give some support to the claim that poetry is not banished *because* it is imitative.

31. The large literature on this subject is well known. A good discussion can be found in Harold Cherniss, "On Plato's *Republic* X 597B," *American Journal of Philology*, 53 (1932), pp. 233–42.

32. paidias charin, I make the following tentative comments.

a. A neglected paper by J. A. Smith ("General Relative Clauses in Greek," *Classical Review*, 31 [1917], pp. 69–71) challenges, on grammatical grounds, the usual translation of 596a6–7, "We are in the habit of postulating one single Form for each plurality of many things to which we give a common name." Smith argues that this translation presupposes that the relative clause, hois tauton onoma epiferomen ("to which we give a common name"), is general, specifying the pluralities to which Forms correspond. But, partly on the authority of William Goodwin, *Syntax of the*

Mood and Tenses of the Greek Verb (Boston: Harvard University Press, 1900), secs. 532, 534, Smith doubts that the clause is general. If it were, he argues, it would have been more correct of Plato to use not hos with indicative, as he does here (and, I add, in another nongeneral clause at 479a1–3), but either hos with subjunctive and an (cf. 479b10) or indicative with hosos or hostis (cf. 426d4–6). If that is so, the "manys" (polla) to which Forms correspond are not defined by the relative clause, but are thought to be known antecedently. Their having a common name is therefore a characteristic that they may share with other groups that are not "manys" in the proper way and to which no Forms correspond. Smith also suggests, however, that tauton should not be translated as "common" (which is the customary translation of koinon) but as "the same" and as referring back to the Form (p. 71). He thus takes tauton onoma ("same name") to carry the implications of, say, homónumon ("homonym," "named after") at *Phd.* 78e2. His version of 596a6–7 would then be something like this: "We are in the habit of postulating one single Form for each group of 'manys'—to which, in that case, we give the same name as that which the Form has." This suggestion, which is not implausible, needs further textual support, especially from a study of Plato's usage of relative clauses—a project much more complicated and systematic than the three instances I produced above, and well beyond the scope of this paper. I thank John J. Keaney for discussing this question with me.

    b. 596a10, thómen dé kai nun hoti boulei tón pollón (Adam's text) is translated, for example, by Shorey, as ". . . let us take any multiplicity you choose." This translation construes the genitive tón pollón as a partitive, and suggests that we are selecting some from among a previously agreed-upon set of "manys." This is a natural reading, but it should not prevent us from seeing that it is possible also to take tón pollón as a genitive of the whole, as in *Laws* 801c5–6: thómen dé kai touton ton peri mousan nomón kai tupón hena; this means: "Shall we set this *as* one among the laws and forms concerning music?" It involves not a selection from, but an addition to, a set. We might then translate 596a10 as follows: "Let us now set whatever you want as among the manys (that is, among those groups to which Forms correspond)." Thus, and consonant with the previous point (a), the generation of Forms of artifacts would be an extension, and not an application, of the usual methods of the Academy. John Cooper has objected that the phrase ho ti boulei tells against this reading. For, he asks, "Are we *really* being asked to extend the theory to *any* direction one wants? No. Rather, only in a *particular* direction." This is true, but I don't think that it dislodges my proposal, for Socrates, who makes this suggestion, immediately goes on to introduce beds and tables, thus securing the direction he wants the argument to take. Glaucon is never allowed to express his own preference.

    c. The Forms of bed and of table may have been chosen by Plato precisely so that, because of their lowliness (atimotés kai faulotés, cf. *Parm.* 130c6–7), the imitator can be put down. These are the very implements that separate the "city of pigs" from the most primitive human city at 372d–e, and are clearly connected with food and with sex—the lowest desires in Plato's scheme. Cf. Charles Griswold's as yet unpublished paper, "The Ideas and the Criticism of Poetry in Plato's *Republic* Book X," p. 8.

    d. That God is the creator of these Forms may appear less incredible (and less in contradiction to *Tim.* 28a–29a, according to which God uses the Forms as patterns) if we recall that these are Forms of artifacts and not of natural objects and kinds, which are what the demiurge of the world uses as his standards. In addition, Socrates' claim that there is a bed "in nature," hén faimen an, hós egómai, theon ergasasthai, involves the potential optative, and could be taken as the rather ironical statement, "We could say, I suppose, that God makes it." Finally, that nothing in Plato's definition of imitation actually depends on God's creating the Forms makes the contradiction (though still not really resolved) less pressing.

33. The painter is said here to imitate both the physical object and the Form (597e1–2). But the point that matters is that the painter produces something distinct from, and consequent upon, the other two. Plato immediately goes on to say that the painter imitates not the Forms but the works of craftsmen (598a1–3).

34. I have supplied an implicit démiourgon despite Adam's claim (*The* Republic *of Plato,* vol. II, p. 392, n. on 597e) that it is unnecessary. The word has already been applied to the painter at 596e6. In the immediately preceding exchange it was claimed that the painter does not make a *bed* (597d11–12), but that he is only an imitator of it (597e1–2). But, as 596e6 has suggested and as the sequel will confirm (cf. 599a1–2, d3), the imitator is a maker of a sort. And the question is: If imitation is making, what is it that it makes?

35. On the difficulties of identifying this king, cf. Adam, *The* Republic *of Plato,* vol. II, pp. 464–65.

36. Plato speaks indifferently of the imitator both as imitating (598b3–4, 600e5) and as making (599a2–3, d3) appearances or images. The significance of this is discussed below, pp. 82–85.

37. It is sometimes claimed that in using the term "phantasm" (fantasma) to describe the objects of painting, Plato is thinking of art that is specifically deceptive and not of art that is true to its model. For example, J. P. Maguire, "The Differentiation of Art in Plato's Aesthetics," *Harvard Studies in Classical Philology,* 68 (1964), pp. 389–410, appeals to *Soph.* 235d–236b, where "eikastic" art, which accurately reproduces its model, is distinguished from "phantastic" art, which does not (pp. 392–93). He writes that "it is the . . . 'phantastic' school which seems to be referred to in *Republic* X and identified with art simply" (p. 393). But the *Sophist* (whose doctrine of images is in many ways different from that of the *Republic*) takes these two as species of a genus, imitation (mimétiké, 235d1). An "eikon" is a species of image (eidólon), which is distinguished by its accuracy; a "phantasm," which is inaccurate, is another. But in its three occurrences in connection with art in the *Republic,* at 401b–c, "eikon" is equivalent to "image" (eidólon, miméma), as also is "phantasm" in Book 10 (see the texts referred to in n. 36). More importantly, Plato's discussion of the deceptiveness of art in Book 10 does not in any way depend on the possible inaccuracy of the representation. He is concerned with the fact that a representation, accurate or inaccurate, may be mistaken for the reality it represents.

38. Plato's procedure is noted by Keuls, "Plato on Painting," but her interests take her in another direction (p. 110).

39. Hermann Koller, *Die Mimesis in der Antike* (Berne: Francke, 1954).

40. Koller, p. 63.

41. Gerald F. Else, "Imitation in the Fifth Century," *Classical Philology,* 53 (1958), pp. 73–90.

42. Koller, p. 37.

43. Else, p. 76.

44. Else, p. 76.

45. Else, p. 77.

46. Else, p. 77; he lists this as a distinct sense of the term on p. 79.

47. We cannot possibly examine all the texts involved in this dispute here. Else seems correct in his view of Aeschylus Fr. 57 Nauck[2] as against Koller (pp. 74–75), but his reconstruction of a hypothetical context that allows him to find in this

"earliest appearance" of *mimos* "an implication which Koller finds nowhere before Plato" (the implication of deception) is much too speculative (pp. 75–76). His view of Pindar *Pythian* 12.21, though possible, does not exclude the sense "reproduce" as opposed to "imitate" for mimésait', so also with his interpretation of Pindar Fr. 94b Snell, l. 15 (p. 77). He interprets Aeschylus Fr. 364 Nauck,[2] liburnikés miméma mandués chitón, as "a shirt that *copies or simulates the appearance* of a Liburnian cloak" (p. 78, my italics). But this imports philosophical presuppositions that the text does not obviously require: "Copied from" or "made like" are not, I think, inappropriate translations. Else's claim that Aeschylus Fr. 190 Mette shows that *mimema* had from its earliest occurrences the connotation of "replica" (p. 78) is correct, though "replica" and "image" (where the latter is taken specifically as "appearance") need not be, as Else supposes, equivalent.

48. Cf. Richard McKeon, "Literary Criticism and the Concept of Imitation in Antiquity," *Modern Philology*, 34 (1936–37), pp. 1–35. For Plato, McKeon writes, "the word 'imitation' indicates the lesser term of the proportion of being to appearance: If God is, the universe is an imitation; if all things are, shadows and reflections are imitations; if the products of man's handicrafts are, his representations of them are imitations" (p. 9).

49. For example, iv. 16: Aryandes wanted to equal (parisoumenos) Darius, so he imitated him (emimeeto) in circulating silver coins in emulation of the king's golden Darians; for this presumption, Aryandes was executed. Similarly, v. 66–68, where Cleisthenes is said to have emulated (emimeeto) his grandfather. We must also note Herodotus' use of *mimesis* to refer to a portrait (iii. 57: mimésis pugmaiou andros).

50. I.95.3. The same is true of VII.63.3. Neither passage, especially the second, carries the suggestion of "aping" that Else claims for them. Cf. Euripides, *Hippolytus* 114, where the old servant claims that he must not imitate (miméteon = act like) the young Hippolytus in not praying to Aphrodite.

51. Else, "Imitation in the Fifth Century," p. 83.

52. The notion of the next best thing also appears in Democritus B38: kalon men ton adikeonta kóluein. ei de mé, mé xunadikeein ("It is noble to stop whoever is acting unjustly; but if not, not to cooperate in the injustice.") Cf. Eric Havelock, *Preface to Plato* (Cambridge, Mass.: Harvard University Press, 1963), p. 58.

53. It is not clear, however, that Euripides *Helen* 74–75 is a good instance of the sense "anything imitated, a counterfeit, copy" under which it is listed in LSJ s.v. miméma: Teucer yells at the real Helen, not realizing who she is, "May the gods spit at you because you are so much (hoson mimém' echeis) like Helen." For other references, cf. Else, "Imitation in the Fifth Century," pp. 79–82.

54. Cf. R. G. Steven, "Plato and the Art of his Time," *Classical Quarterly*, 27 (1933), pp. 149–55, esp. p. 150.

55. Plato has already mentioned painting in connection with a contrast between appearance and reality at 583b and 586b–c. For a discussion of Plato's overall attitude toward painting in the *Republic*, cf. Nancy Demand, "Plato and the Painters," *Phoenix*, 29 (1975), pp. 1–20. Demand finds his treatment of painting in Book 10 harsher than, and inconsistent with, his treatment in earlier books, and explains this discrepancy by the hypothesis that *Republic* 10 was composed considerably later than the first nine books of the work. We have seen that this is also the view of Else, *The Structure and Date of Book 10 of Plato's Republic*.

56. For an extreme but provocative statement of this view, cf. Havelock, *Preface to Plato*.

57. Plotinus, *Enneads*, V.viii.1. John Dillon has pointed out to me that Plotinus may have been influenced by Cicero, *Orator* ii.8–10.

58. M. H. Abrams, *The Mirror and the Lamp: Romantic Theory and the Critical*

Tradition (New York: Oxford University Press, 1953), pp. 42–44; Monroe C. Beardsley, *Aesthetics: Problems in the Philosophy of Criticism* (New York: Harcourt, Brace & Company, 1958), p. 394.

59. For example, David Daiches, *Critical Approaches to Literature* (Englewood Cliffs, N.J.: Prentice-Hall, 1956): "Why it did not occur to Plato that the painter, by painting the *ideal* object, could suggest the ideal form and thus make direct contact with reality . . . is not easy to see," p. 20. Cf. also Grube, *Plato's Thought*, p. 202.

60. The literature on this question is enormous.

Some scholars think that good art imitates Forms and is still recognizably art. Such is the view of Tate, " 'Imitation' in Plato's *Republic*," pp. 21–22, and "Plato and 'Imitation,' " pp. 164–65; Leon Golden, "Plato's Concept of Mimesis," *British Journal of Aesthetics*, 15 (1975), pp. 118–31; Victor Goldschmidt, "Le problème de la tragédie d'après Platon," *Questions Platoniciennes* (Paris: J. Vrin, 1970), pp. 103–40; Henri Joly, *Le Renversement Platonicien* (Paris: J. Vrin, 1974); Iris Murdoch, *The Fire and the Sun*; Carritt, *The Theory of Beauty*, esp. pp. 31–32; Greene, "Plato's View of Poetry," pp. 34–35; Maguire, "The Differentiation of Art in Plato's Aesthetics," p. 394; R. C. Lodge, *Plato's Theory of Art* (London: Routledge & Kegan Paul, 1953), p. 182.

Some of these join other scholars in believing that Plato's objections to art are only objections to the art of his time on the grounds that it is too realistic and illusionistic. Cf. Cherniss, "On Plato's *Republic* X 597B," p. 241; Greene, "Plato's View of Poetry," p. 54; Nettleship, *Lectures on the Republic of Plato*, p. 353; Friedländer, *Plato*, vol. I, p. 119; Tate, "Plato and 'Imitation,' " pp. 164–65. The idea that Plato attacks not art in general but only the art of his time (with or without reference to the theory of Forms) has been much discussed by historians of Greek painting. The classic work by Pierre-Maxim Schuhl, *Platon et l'art de son temps* (*Arts Plastiques*), 2d ed. (Paris, 1952) established the picture of Plato as a forceful participant in a *"lutte entre les anciens et les modernes"*; cf. Steven, "Plato and the Art of his Time." Different views have recently been expressed by Keuls, "Plato on Painting," who connects what she considers of Plato's gradually increasing distaste for the plastic arts with the rise of the scientific pretensions of the Sicyonian school, and by Demand, "Plato and the Painters." My own view is that this debate has assumed proportions greater than those it deserves since Plato, at least in *Republic* 10, does not banish the painters and since, as Demand herself shows, his earlier references to painting in the *Republic* are not as pejorative as it is often thought.

Other scholars, again, believe that true art is really philosophy—for example, Oates, *Plato's View of Art*, p. 40; David Gallop, "Image and Reality in Plato's *Republic*," *Archiv für Geschichte der Philosophie*, 47 (1965), pp. 113–31. Those scholars who think that Plato's dialogues constitute true poetry also seem to me to accept such a view—for example, Friedländer, *Plato*, vol. I, pp. 118–22; Partee, "Plato's Banishment of Poetry," p. 219. The objection to this view is mainly that it establishes what it seeks to avoid—that there is no *poetry*, or *art*, that imitates Forms.

61. " 'Imitation' in Plato's *Republic*," p. 18; cf. p. 21. So also Shorey, *The Republic of Plato*, vol. I, p. 260 n. *a*. On *Rep.* 401c see also Verdenius, *Mimesis*, p. 14.

62. Adam, *The Republic of Plato*, vol. I, p. 168, n. on 402c. Contrast further the plurals ta tés sófrosunés eidé (the forms of temperance, etc.) with the emphasis on the uniqueness of each eidos at, for example, 476aff.

63. Tate, " 'Imitation' in Plato's *Republic*," p. 21. But contrast Shorey, *The Republic of Plato*, vol. I, p. 504 n. *a*.

64. So Gallop, "Image and Reality in Plato's *Republic*," p. 116, and Adam, *The Republic of Plato*, vol. I, p. 328, n. on 472d. Contrast again Shorey, ibid.

65. Tate, "Plato, Art, and Mr. Maritain," p. 111, claims that 599d and 607a show "that genuine art is once removed (not twice) from the ideal world." But 599d simply says that if Homer had been only once removed from reality, then he would have known what makes people truly virtuous, and would have functioned as a legislator. The reference to 607a is even less convincing.

66. So Tate, "Plato and 'Imitation,' " p. 167.

67. Cf. Epicurus, *ap.* Diogenes Laertius X.xxvi.121: "Only the wise man will have the right view of music and poetry: And he will live, not write, poems" (monon te ton sofon orthós an peri te mousikés kai poiétikés dialexesthai. poiémata te energein, ouk an poiésai.).

68. For Example, Tate, " 'Imitation' in Plato's *Republic*," p. 22.

69. Cf. Charles M. Young, "A Note on *Republic* 335c9–10 and 335c12," *Philosophical Review*, 83 (1974), pp. 97–106, esp. pp. 104–5.

70. I am indebted to Paul Woodruff for discussing this issue with me.

71. The term is used at *Tim.* 48e2, but it is a notorious fact that Plato never settled exactly what that relationship was.

72. No mention is made of imitation at *Crat.* 388a–389a, the only other passage where Plato describes the making of artifacts in terms of looking at the Forms.

73. Often this is not noticed, but the point is made by J. P. Vernant, "Image dans la théorie Platonicienne de Mimèsis," *Journal de Psychologie*, 2 (1975), pp. 133–60; " . . . *l'Idée de lit ne peut être imitée de cette façon* (that in which the sensible bed is imitated by the artist). *Son rapport avec le lit du menuisier n'est pas homologue à la semblance de ce dernier avec l'image du peintre . . .*" (p. 158).

74. Cf. Vernant, pp. 139–41, and Collingwood, "Plato's Philosophy of Art," *Mind*, 34 (1925), pp. 154–72, esp. p. 158.

75. Collingwood, "Plato's Philosophy of Art," p. 159. A more extreme view is that of Walter Pater, *Plato and Platonism* (New York: Macmillan, 1894), who, on the basis of *Rep.* 341d, found that Plato anticipates the doctrine of art for art's sake (p. 241).

76. With Socrates' comment here that people don't seem to be able to compose both tragedies and comedies, compare his position in the *Symposium* that comedy and tragedy actually should be written by the same author (223d). It is interesting to recall in this connection the many parts that each actor in a Greek drama would have to play.

77. On the background of Plato's attitude, cf. Gregory Vlastos, "Degrees of Reality in Plato," in Renford Bambrough (ed.), *New Essays on Plato and Aristotle* (London: Routledge & Kegan Paul, 1965), pp. 1–19.

78. Cf. Terence Irwin, *Plato's Moral Theory* (New York: Oxford University Press, 1977), pp. 73–75.

79. To avoid a possible misunderstanding, I should say that nothing said above implies that two different paintings of Socrates, since both are of Socrates, are identical to each other. The two paintings can be quite distinct frescoes, or canvases, or what have you—but they are identical as *paintings*, according to this view, since their content is the same. In addition, their quality, on this view, can vary in accordance to the degree of their likeness to their model.

80. To Plato's statement compare, ironically, the following: "Art is not the most precious manifestation of life. Art has not the celestial and universal value that people like to attribute to it. Life is far more interesting." This is the view of Tristan Tzara, "Lecture on Dada," in Robert Motherwell, *The Dada Painters and Poets* (New York: Wittenborn, Schultz, 1951), p. 248.

81. A similar point is made in the additional argument at 601b9–602b5, where *mimesis* is called craft or art (techné). Still, it is no more an art than the bed the painter makes is a bed (with "three arts," treis technas, at 601d1, cp. "three beds,"

trittai klinai at 597b5). This argument involves the claim that at least in some cases knowledge and belief have the same object (for example, cf. 601e5–6), and this seems to contradict the epistemology developed in Book 5. But see Gail Fine, "Knowledge and Belief in *Republic* V," *Archiv für Geschichte der Philosophie*, 60 (1978), pp. 121–39.

82. Some of its complications are noticed by N. R. Murphy, *The Interpretation of Plato's* Republic (Oxford: Clarendon Press, 1951), pp. 239–43.

83. Cf. Terry Penner, "Thought and Desire in Plato," in Gregory Vlastos (ed.), *Plato II: Ethics, Politics, and Philosophy of Art and Religion* (Garden City, N.Y.: Doubleday & Company, 1971), p. 100.

84. Murphy, *The Interpretation of Plato's* Republic, p. 241.

85. Adam, who accepts this traditional view himself, notes this as a difficulty, *The* Republic *of Plato*, vol. II, p. 406, n. on 602cff. Penner, "Thought and Desire in Plato," is not disturbed by this fact, since it is part of his view that the appetitive part of the soul does engage in (rudimentary)thought (pp. 100–1).

86. Cf. John M. Cooper, "Plato's Theory of Human Motivation," unpublished, and Gary Watson, "Free Agency," *Journal of Philosophy*, 72 (1975), pp. 205–20.

87. Cf. John M. Cooper, "The Theory of Good in Plato's *Philebus*," unpublished, p. 41.

88. Penner, "Thought and Desire in Plato," p. 113.

89. Cooper, "Plato's Theory of Human Motivation."

90. "Irascible" (aganaktétikon) is connected with spirit and emotion via "rage" (orgé) and "raging" (orgizesthai) at 440a5, d2; "variable" (poikilon) is connected with appetite via poikilou at 588c7 and polueidia at 580d11.

91. John Jones, *On Aristotle and Greek Tragedy* (New York: Oxford University Press, 1962), p. 44, my italics.

92. From a very different point of view, Marshall Cohen tries to show that art does not always involve distance and that it *does* have a direct effect on its audience ("Aesthetic Essence," in George Dickie and R. J. Sclafani, *Aesthetics: A Critical Anthology* [New York: St. Martin's Press, 1977]). He writes (pp. 487–88) that "the muzzles of the battleship *Potemkin*, pointed at the audience, are positively menacing." *Positively*, perhaps: but *really*?

93. On the strong reaction of Greek audiences to poetic recitation, cf. *Odyssey* viii.521ff, Xenophon *Symposium* iii.11, *Ion* 535c–e. On naturalism in Greek acting style, cf. Peter Walcot, *Greek Drama in Its Theatrical and Social Context* (Cardiff: University of Wales Press, 1976), ch. 5.

94. *Rep.* 607e–608b uses the violent language of *Phaedrus* 255b–256b to describe the lover of poetry and his fight against giving in to it.

95. Cf. *Laws* 801e1–4, which makes essentially the same point. Considering the *Laws*' use of "prayers" (euchai) and Socrates' own description of his prayer to Pan at the end of the *Phaedrus* as an euché (279b6–c7), it does not seem to me such a view as Collingwood's, *The Principles of Art*, p. 48, is correct. On "praise" (enkómion) see *Symp.* 177a–b, and the speeches that make up the bulk of that dialogue.

96. Cf. Thomas Gould, "Plato's Hostility to Poetry," *Arion*, 3 (1964), pp. 70–91. Since Plato's hostility is, if my argument is correct, very specific, Gould's diagnosis, which appeals to what he considers Plato's all-embracing systematic dualism, can be challenged. Still, Gould stresses correctly that Plato was unwilling to make any serious exception to his banishment of poetry. Cf. also Murphy, *The Interpretation of Plato's* Republic, p. 224; and, of course, Havelock, *Preface to Plato*, passim.

CHAPTER IV

"This Story Isn't True": Poetry, Goodness, and Understanding in Plato's *Phaedrus*

Martha Craven Nussbaum

> When one is young, one venerates and despises without that art
> of nuances which constitutes the best gain of life, and it is only
> fair that one has to pay dearly for having assaulted men and
> things in this manner with Yes and No. Everything is arranged so
> that the worst of tastes, the taste for the unconditional, should be
> cruelly fooled and abused until a man learns to put a little art into
> his feelings and rather to risk trying even what is artificial—as
> the real artists of life do.
>
> Nietzsche, *Beyond Good and Evil*, 31 (tr. Kaufmann)

"My dear friend Phaedrus, where are you going and where do you come from?" So begins what I shall claim to be a self-critical and questioning dialogue. Phaedrus says that he has come from talking with Lysias, son of Cephalus. (Immediately we are reminded of the *Republic*, in which both father and son were characters and which took place, in fact, in their house.) He is going from the urban house where he has been conversing with Lysias to take a walk outside the city walls, in what we shall shortly see to be a place of burgeoning sensuous beauty. In the same way, certain important features of Plato's thought and writing seem to have left the house of the *Republic* and to be moving off in the direction of greater wildness, perhaps even sensuousness. This chapter will try to ask Socrates' questions of Plato: Where does he come from here, and where is he going?[1]

Fact 1. In the *Republic*, Socrates makes a sharp distinction between poetry and philosophy. He attacks poetry for nourishing the irrational parts of the soul, repudiates its claim to illuminate the truth, and contrasts the cognitive deficiency of the poet with the philosopher's wisdom. In the *Phaedrus*, the highest life is described as one devoted to either philosophical or Muse-honoring activities; poetry inspired by "madness" is defended as a gift of the gods, and an invaluable educational resource. Socrates presents his deepest philosophical insights in poetic language, in the form of a "likeness."

Fact 2. In the *Republic*, the irrational appetites and emotions, particularly the erotic appetite, are held to be unsuitable guides for human action. Only reason can guide man toward the good. Socrates claims that what I really am is an incorruptible reason, only contingently linked with the appetitive and desiderative elements, and therefore separable, both logically and historically, from appetitive and emotional desires. Lasting erotic relationships between individuals do not seem to be important elements in the good life. In the *Phaedrus*, philosophy itself is said to be a form of *mania*—of "possessed," not purely rational activity, in which reason is guided to insight by the cognitive work of erotic longing. My "real nature" is seen to be complex, not simple. Erotic relationships of long duration between particular individuals are seen to be both fundamental in psychological development and an important component of the best human life.

Fact 3. In the *Republic*, the culmination of philosophical growth is the achievement of a nonanthropocentric understanding of the world, a grasp of things as they really are in themselves, unconditioned by merely human interests and ways of seeing. "Nothing incomplete is ever the measure of anything" (*Rep.* 504c). The *Phaedrus* denies that the whole and unconditioned truth is available, as such, to any human being. It introduces, as fundamental to dialectic, a method of analysis that seems to direct us toward the more exact elucidation of the "appearances"—what we, as humans and as language users, say and believe.

Fact 4. In the *Phaedrus*, Socrates covers his head in shame and, uncovering it, recants a stern prose discourse that had attacked *erōs* as a form of degrading madness and described the appetites as mere urges for bodily replenishment, with no role to play in our understanding of the good. His recantation takes the form of a poetic quotation. He recites the Palinode of Stesichorus, who had slandered Helen and, struck blind for his error, composed these verses to regain his sight:

This story isn't true.
You did not embark on the well-benched ships.
You did not come to the citadel of Troy.

It is the plan of this chapter to explore the connections among these suggestive facts. I shall argue that the *Phaedrus* is indeed more hospitable to poetry and the poet than the *Republic*, and less certain about the distinction between poetry and philosophy. These changes can best be explained as growing out of a more pervasive shift in Plato's moral psychology. I shall argue that the *Phaedrus* both implicitly criticizes and formally recants some views about the appetites and emotions, about the components of the good life, and about personal identity that had been seriously defended in the *Phaedo* and *Republic*. Finally, I shall explore the connection between this shift in position and the dialogue's new epistemological/metaphysical direction.

Before we begin, it may be in order to comment further on Fact 4. It should by now be clear that I plan to find some striking resemblances between the doctrine of Socrates' first speech and some views seriously defended by Socrates in middle-period dialogues: the recantation is a serious recantation of something Plato has seriously endorsed. The resemblances will, later, speak for themselves; and I hope it will emerge that the prevailing opinion that finds this speech (and the related speech of Lysias) degrading, disgusting, and unworthy has failed to see how difficult it is to say this while regarding with sympathy the asceticism of the *Phaedo*. The early speeches are serious and plausible; in certain moods one is convinced of their truth. But one reason they have been lightly regarded—one reason why my interpretation will, no doubt, be resisted—is that Socrates himself expresses here his shame and disgust. He utters them under a kind of compulsion, and quickly recants, claiming they said what was neither healthy nor true (242c). What, then, within the *Phaedrus* itself, could persuade us to think of them as serious competitors for Socrates' own allegiance?

First, respect for their author. I do not believe that Plato ever criticizes a straw man, or that he would spend so much time on a position that he finds simply worthless or disgusting, to which a reasonable man would not be seriously drawn. But there is also more specific evidence. The speeches are criticized, first and foremost, for their naïveté (*euētheia,* 242d7, e5); this is an odd thing to say about something one views as cynical, debased, and altogether without hope or interest. Second, and more telling, Socrates claims that it was his *daimonion,* his "divine sign," that prompted the recantation. The *daimonion* is a serious individual, who intercedes infrequently to "hold back" Socrates when he is about to undertake something wrong (*Phdr.* 242c, cf. *Apol.* 31d). Even making allowances for Socratic irony, we would not expect it to intervene when Socrates is in no way genuinely tempted to the wrong view or choice, when he is, in fact, merely role playing. Another indication of seriousness is provided by the fact that Socrates' first speech is said to be inspired by certain Muses—not, to be sure, the Pan, Nymphs, and gods of wild nature who inspire his later discourse (cf. 279bc, 262d, 263de), but certain Muses of the "clear voiced" Ligurian variety. We might call them Muses of rationalism, or the Muses of the middle dialogues. As Hackforth points out, the presence of Muses here "creates a real difficulty" for those who are inclined to be abruptly dismissive of the first speech.[2]

Finally, a strange feature of the first speech itself, not readily explicable on the usual assumptions, gives us a hint about the continuity between Socrates' two speeches. The speech denouncing *erōs* is said to be the speech of a lover to his beloved boy. This lover, however, pretends he is not a lover and speaks slandering *erōs,* urging his beloved not to yield to the lover's importunities. This strange bit of byplay is explained by Hackforth as a sign that the speaker is motivated by real concern for the boy's welfare. "In fact, we get a glimpse of the *erastēs* par excellence, Socrates himself."[3] This promising line of interpretation can be developed much further if we take the content of the speech more seriously than Hackforth has, as an expression of Plato's own views. Here is a lover who tells us, apparently sincerely, that *erōs* is a madness and a disease; anyone for whom he cares should avoid its grip and seek to live in reason with reasonable people. It would not be difficult to see the ascetic arguments of the *Phaedo* and the *Republic* as the speech of such a lover, a lover convinced that, in order to lead toward the good both himself and his readers, he must not only attack the passions but also pretend that he himself is not a profoundly erotic personality. He might even pretend to be Socrates, who was impervious to drink, to cold, to fatigue, to the naked body of Alcibiades. In the person of this same Socrates, Plato elsewhere tells us that a man in love, if he thinks that *erōs* is not good for him, continually rehearses to himself the arguments against *erōs* as a "countercharm" to her spell. Even so, Plato continues, a lover of poetry should rehearse to himself the arguments against this form of madness—unless and until a defender of poetry should convince him "in prose without meter, and show that she is not only delightful but beneficial to orderly government and all the life of man" (*Rep.* 607d–608b).

The *Phaedrus* begins to look like it may be this *apologia*, following upon some of the most powerful countercharms a philosopher and lover has ever spoken to himself and to us. One senses that Plato's work is, all through, the work of an erotic man and a lover of poetry—even, and especially, in its denunciations. The *Phaedrus* would then be a place of acknowledgment, in which the mature Plato admits that he has been blind to something, conceived oppositions too starkly and without shading; where he seeks, through acceptance of his complex human nature and mixed intellectual gifts, to get back his sight.

I. POETRY

In a number of dialogues traditionally assigned to the "early" and "middle" period of his work,[4] Plato sharply contrasts the poet and the philosopher, and rejects the claim of the former to genuine understanding. There is, he tells us, "an old difference" or "opposition" between poetry and philosophy (*Rep.* 607b). The poet is characterized consistently in the *Apology*, the *Ion*, the *Meno*, and the tenth book of the *Republic*, as a person who works in a state of irrational possession or transport, and whose creations are expressive of this state.[5] They are "in a state of frenzied enthusiasm" (*enthousiōntes, Apol., Meno*); they "hold their bacchic revels" (*bakcheuousi, Ion*); they are "inspired" (*epipnoi, Meno*), "god inspired" (*entheoi, Ion*), "not in their senses" (*ouch emphrones, Ion*), "possessed" (*katechomenoi, Meno, Ion*). This irrational state is contrasted with the self-possessed good sense of the philosopher, who is in a cognitive position to answer questions and give accounts. (It is assumed, usually without further argument, that the possessed are, just because of their possession, unable to satisfy the philosopher's demand.) Since Plato always ties the notion of *epistēmē,* or understanding,[6] very closely to the ability to give accounts or explanations, the poets, inasmuch as they lack this ability, are said to lack understanding. They may, by accident, speak the truth, but "they know nothing of what they say" (*Apol., Meno*—in identical words). A "good poet" would have to create with understanding (*eidota poiein*) if he were going to create well. Otherwise he wouldn't be able to create (*Rep.* 598e).

Evidently, then, Plato's criticism of the poet depends on:

1. a claim that poets create out of an irrational state of the personality akin to inspiration or madness;
2. a claim that someone in such a state is, *eo ipso,* unable to give a satisfactory *logos* of what he discusses;
3. a claim that the ability to produce an adequate *logos* is a necessary condition of *epistēmē;*
4. a claim that teaching that does not embody *epistēmē* is worthless as moral teaching.

Plato's repeated claim that the poet deals in "appearances," seen in the context of these claims, need not mean anything so bizarre as that the poet confuses the painting of a man with a real man, the dramatized courageous action with a real action—or that he tries to foist this confusion on us. It may mean, rather, that, lacking the systematic understanding of courage or of man that would issue in the sort of *logos* that could satisfy a philosopher's demand for inclusiveness, generality, and reason-giving explanatory adequacy, he is doomed to float about in a realm of mere conjecture.[7] He depicts things the way they strike him, without clear criteria or clear boundaries. His portrayal of courage might be "true": he might, that is, in a particular case, hit on the sort of courageous act that would, to the philosopher, be an acceptable or even an instructive example. But he tells this truth by accident, because he has not done the sort of reflective sorting out of "appearances" that would put them in a coherent order and enable him to reject some spurious pretenders to the title. Insofar as we follow, and are taught by, the play of his disorderly imagination, we will be similarly defective.

Plato has a further, separable criticism of the mimetic poet. Unlike the philosopher, who addresses himself to the *logistikon,* the pure, calculating and measuring, value-determining reason, the poet addresses himself to, and thereby nourishes, the irrational elements in the soul. He finds that the irrational presents him with his best opportunities for interesting poetry; excessive displays of feeling are especially moving to his audience (*Rep.* 604e–605a). But, by presenting in his work emotions like grief and erotic love, he feeds and strengthens the irrational parts of soul in them, jeopardizing their efforts at rational control (cf. *Rep.* 386a–388e, 605b, 606a, 606d, 607a).

At first we might think that this criticism is simply an application of the preceding one: What is bad about the way poetry treats the emotions is that it is not able to give a *logos* of them, a systematic account of when and how they are appropriately felt and expressed. But we soon see that there is more to the point than this. Plato has good reason for asserting the argument that divided the soul into "parts" has enabled us to produce a deeper criticism of poetry than we could make in Book 3 (595ab). First, Plato is assuming that the display of bad emotional and appetitive behavior itself encourages and strengthens such behavior, whether accompanied by a *logos* of its badness or not. Even if the poet were in possession of the philosopher's *logos,* it would presumably be *bad* for the poet to represent bad examples, even as examples of badness. Plato believes with reason that without bad and excessive characters representational poetry will lose much of its interest. With no excessive behavior and no conflict between good and bad, there could, for instance, be no tragedy. Second (and this is the point that will more seriously occupy us in what follows), for Plato a good deal—indeed, most—of our emotional and appetitive behavior is, just be being that, bad. Certain very common emotions are necessarily linked with false beliefs and valuations. Grief, for example, is linked with false beliefs about the mortality of the soul and with pernicious misestimations of the importance of human life; the fear of death, again, with a false eschatology; erotic love, as usually experienced and as depicted in poetry, with false beliefs about the uniqueness and irreplaceability of the loved one's beauty.[8] But these are the emotions that lie at the heart of tragedy; moral indignation, anger at the enemy—these manifestations of *thumos,* though permissible, are not enough to keep a drama going.

So all representational poetry, at any rate, is to be rejected—not only because of its failure to embody a systematic understanding of the good, but also because of its unhealthy relationship to the irrational. Philosophical discourse, on the other hand, is praised for its ability to produce general truths, and for addressing itself wholesomely to pure reason alone. Plato allows, indeed, that the debate is not yet over. Socrates does, as we saw, invite the lover of poetry to convince him that his story is not true (607de). But such a rebuttal, to be successful, would clearly have to address itself not merely to aesthetic issues, but also to the central questions in moral psychology and moral theory that underlie the *Republic*'s criticism. In particular, we would expect the rebuttal to be concerned with two issues: (1) the necessity of a certain sort of *logos* for genuine understanding; and (2) the strong distinction between the rational and irrational parts of the soul and the denial of cognitive efficacy to the latter.

From the very beginning of the *Phaedrus,* we suspect that some such rebuttal is either presupposed or in progress. Phaedrus asks Socrates whether he believes that the myth of Boreas is true (229c). Socrates, in answer, speaks harshly of some "wise men" (*sophoi,* 229c) who doubt the truth of myths, and cleverly invent (*sophizomenoi)* rationalizing explanations for the origins of stories. Although the idea that myths and stories may convey truths has appeared in Plato's writing before, it fits uneasily with his attacks on literature and his demand for a certain kind of universal explanatory *logos.* In fact, the most eloquent pre-*Phaedrus* exponent of the view that one can tell the truth through stories and images is Alcibiades in the *Symposium,* a character whose views are both unacceptable to Socrates and seen to be connected with a "mad," disorderly way of life. Socrates in that dialogue depicts the philosopher as advancing ever farther away from the particularity of story and image, toward the most general understanding of the unitary essence of all beauty.[9] Although the rationalizer of the *Phaedrus* is probably not the philosopher of the *Republic* and *Symposium*, it is still somewhat surprising to find Socrates here defending the insights of traditional stories against what he calls a "rustic wisdom" (229d), the work of "an excessively clever and hard-working and not entirely fortunate man" (229d4).

The next surprise comes in Socrates' criticism of the prose speech of Lysias, where the orator is praised for clarity and conciseness, but scolded for (among other faults) his apparent lack of interest in the subject matter (235a). Again, we remember that poets were criticized precisely because they wrote in a state of passionate arousal; their exposition of the truth was alleged to be perverted by their interest.

But none of this, suggestive though it is, would lead us to conclude that something new is going on if it were not for the way poetry figures in Socrates' second speech. Socrates announces at the outset that the speech is the speech of "Stesichorus son of Euphemus, of Himera" (244a). These names are significant. Euphemus, "reverent in speech," seems to refer to the speech's respectful treatment of *erōs*, against which the earlier speeches had blasphemed (242e–243b). The earlier speeches were a "slander" (*kakēgoria,* 243a6); the later one finds Socrates in a state of "fear and shame before the divinity of *erōs*" (243d), eagerly desirous of purifying himself (243a, d) with the water of appropriate speech. But this pious speech is, at the same time, the work of a poet, "Stesichorus," and of a man from Himera—from a place that we may call Longington or Passionville. Socrates thus tells us, by the use of a poetic figure of speech, that the reverent and healthy speech is the speech of a poet and a needy lover; and, furthermore, that he is that poet.

The yearning speech opens with a defense of irrational *mania* and an attack on the simple dichotomy between madness and self-possession used by the first two speeches to discredit the lover. (We shall study this attack further below.) Four forms of madness are praised as sources of the highest goods. The third is described as follows:

> Third is the possession (*katokochē*) and madness (*mania*) from the Muses, which, taking a tender and pure soul, awakens it and makes it join the bacchic revels (*ekbakcheuousa*), in lyric and in

other kinds of poetry as well; adorning countless deeds of our ancestors it instructs posterity. Whoever comes to the gates of poetry without the madness of the Muses, persuaded that he will be an adequate poet from craft *(technē)* alone, he and his poetry, being those of a self-possessed *(sōphronountos)* person, come to nothing and are eclipsed. [245b]

There can now be little doubt that Socrates means here to praise as a possible source of great good something that he had previously argued to be generally detrimental to the soul and incompatible with genuine understanding. All the key words of the earlier criticisms reappear, now with a positive connotation. *Katokochē* elsewhere designated the bad irrationality of the poet who, in the grip of feeling, could not produce a *logos*. And *mania* has been used in the *Republic* and other earlier dialogues with an exclusively pejorative connotation, to pick out the bad state of soul in which the irrational parts, especially appetite, are dominant over reason.[10] When this speech acknowledges the inspired poet's claim to bring a great good, *not* in spite of, but *because of* his *mania,* when it even ranks him far above the poet who works in a self-possessed, *sōphrōn* way through the principles of *technē*, we begin to feel that the recantation is a recantation indeed. It then comes as no surprise to find that when Socrates later ranks lives in order of their excellence, the first place is occupied by a strange hybrid: "a man who will be a lover of wisdom or a lover of beauty or some follower of the Muses[11] and a lover" (248d). In the world of the *Republic,* when lives are ranked, the philosopher is alone at the top. Certainly he does not share his berth with unsavory, inspired bacchic types like the poet and the lover. His own sort of *erōs* is sharply distinguished from theirs. Now philosopher, poet, lover—all are seen as inspired types, and inspiration comes at the top.[12] A philosopher is delivering the speech of Stesichorus from Passionville. Everything seems upside down. Now we are even told that it makes no difference whether we call the highest type "the one who philosophizes without guile" or "the one who pursues the love of boys along with philosophy" (248a). Before, it would have made all the difference.

It is unlikely that these changes would lead to a rehabilitation of the poets whose work Plato knew. Philosophical activity still seems to be necessary for the highest sort of understanding; it is also necessary for the best sort of love (cf. esp. 249c), and, as we shall see, for the best sort of devotion to the Muses. The disjunction, "*either* a lover of wisdom *or* a lover of beauty *or* some follower of the Muses" probably does not imply that any one of these, without the others, would be sufficient. The point is, rather, that they are taken, as they could not have been before, to be compatible—perhaps even, in their highest realizations, to imply one another. (It doesn't matter which of these names you call him, because if he's one, he's the others too.) The speech about madness has already dismissed the uninspired poet; and in the list of lives the ordinary *poiētēs* (who is not said to be Muse-inspired) comes in sixth place, quite far down the ladder (248e). Later we are told that Homer will be permitted the title of philosopher only if he can show his understanding by answering questions about his writing (278c); but this, as the *Apology* already told us, is something actual poets are unable to do.

So the change implies no softening toward the nonphilosophical poet. The really significant point, however, is that philosophy is now permitted to be an inspired, manic, Muse-loving activity. And in this conception it is much more intimately related to poetry than Plato has hitherto led us to think. (It might, for example, make use of "literary" devices such as mythic narrative and metaphor; and it might, like poetry, contain material expressive of, and arousing in turn, a passional excitation.) The rest of the dialogue confirms this close relationship. At the conclusion of Socrates' speech (a speech that he praises as *more beautiful* than the preceding), Phaedrus is called a "lover of the Muses" *(philomouson andra)*. The myth of the cicadas that follows tells us that philosophy, along with the dance and erotic love, is one of the arts that made its appearance in the world with the advent of the Muses. The philosophical life is said to be a life dedicated to "Calliope and Urania"—that is, to the Muse traditionally associated with poetry, as well as to the mother of cosmology (259bc). (We notice that ordinary poetry is *not* mentioned as an art genuinely inspired by the Muses; this is consistent with the low placement of the mere *poiētēs* before, and with the distinction between this person and the higher *mousikos*. The poet does not genuinely serve the Muses

if he does not join his art with philosophy.) And, at the dialogue's
end, the philosopher's message to Homer tells him that Socrates
and Phaedrus have heard the words they relay from the "stream
and Music haunt *(mouseion)* of the Nymphs." What the Nymphs
told them is that poetry is philosophy if it is combined in the right
way with answers and accounts.

What we see emerging, then, is not so much a rehabilitation of
the old poetry, as a new understanding of philosophy that reinter-
prets the distinction between philosophy and poetry; not so much
an acceptance of Homer's innocence of *logoi,* as an announcement
that philosophy, like Socrates, may have a more complex soul than
had been imagined.

But we do not need to rely only on explicit metaphilosophical
remarks to know this, for Plato's praise of the inspired poet profoundly affects the shape of his own discourse. The speech of the
poet from Himera is still a prose speech. And it does not employ
internal dramatic representation in its depiction of the lovers who
are its characters. It even contains a section that is in the form of a
formal demonstrative argument and is called such by Socrates
(245c). But there is no doubt that, more than any other Platonic
speech we have so far encountered, this clearly is the speech of an
inspired philosopher-poet. It uses metaphor, personification, col-
orful, rhythmic, and elaborate language. It makes its appeal to the
imagination and the feelings as much as to the reason; or, rather, it
makes us wonder how legitimate it is to separate these so starkly.
Although the first part of the exposition that claims to reveal the
"truth" about the soul's nature (245c) is a demonstration, the
second and much longer part takes the form of a "likeness": the
picture of the horses and the charioteer, which gives us an intuitive
sense of what our souls are like. Socrates is a philosopher who,
being, as he says, only human, cannot give a definition of the soul
(246a); but he regards his ability to produce a likeness as sufficient
to give him the right to call himself a lover of wisdom and a teacher.
Only a god could do better. So it may be that the class of *logoi*
yielding understanding is a more varied class than Plato has previously acknowledged; it may include stories, likenesses, things that
can be produced, and are best produced by madmen.[13]

This dialogue, then, may be our first example of the philosophical poetry Plato has in mind; perhaps nobody has ever served the two muses adequately together, been a *mousikos* instead of a mere *poiētēs*. And what Plato tells us is that we cannot throw away the images as delightful decorations, or lift out his arguments from their "literary" context for isolated dissection. The whole thing is a Music discourse, and to understand Plato's thought requires undertanding how this is so.

This is a thought to which Plato criticism, and philosophy generally, has been remarkably resistant. The tendency to regard arguments as expressing the content of a philosophy, image, story, and conversation as giving it a pleasing, decorative surface goes very deep in our entire philosophical tradition. Philosophy has developed style for itself that powerfully expresses its claim to have separated the rational from the irrational, to have purified itself of the confusions of emotion and sense, which are the stuff of poetic discourse. The deductive argument keeps these messy irrational elements at bay, protecting reason's structures against them. It is evident that the question of philosophical style is connected at a very deep level with a conception of the rational and of the relation between "rational" and "irrational." Plato's writing tells us, in its multifaceted progress, that these questions need to be reopened, these polarities re-examined. To read him as we most commonly do—searching for system *beneath* story, numbered premises *at the bottom of* an image—is to miss the opportunity to ask ourselves some of the most interesting and deep questions that his text opens up for us. It is a dangerous business to allow ourselves to ask them, since this threatens to call our entire way of life, our practices of teaching and writing, into question. Who can risk the discovery that Music abilities and responses, elements of the person not frequently cultivated by our graduate schools of philosophy, might be an important, even essential, part of writing genuine philosophy? (That most philosophical articles might be productions of *sōphrosunē thnētē,* mortal self-possession, rather than philosophical inspiration?) So we keep the "literary," and Plato's styles, at bay; we write about him using the very conception of pure philosophical or analytic skill that the *Phaedrus* is calling into question. (Or, what is certainly much worse, far more a betrayal of Plato's project, we acknowledge only this other aspect of Plato, and take to writing works of paradox and image play that explain nothing, argue nothing, and have not even the grace of Homer to commend them.)

II. MORAL PSYCHOLOGY

Something, clearly, is going on. But by now it is clear that in order to understand this something, in order to see what Plato is saying about philosophy and its style, we must go more deeply into the question of madness and *sōphrosunē,* asking what *mania* is and what Plato means by the claim that it is not a "simple evil" and can be the source of the highest good. Muse inspiration becomes philosophical in the course of Socrates' renunciation of simple psychological dichotomy between bad madness and good *sōphrosunē.* We need to know on what grounds *mania* has been too simply blamed, and how, and to what degree, it now finds its way back into the good life.

A. MADNESS

What is madness or possession? Consistently in pre-*Phaedrus* dialogues, Plato has used these words of the state of the soul in which the irrational elements—appetites and emotions—are in control and lead or guide the rational part. It is consistently, as here, contrasted with *sōphrosunē,* the state of soul in which reason rules securely over the irrational elements. (It is linked particularly with the dominance of the erotic appetite.)[14] The madman is, then, a person who is in the sway of inner forces that, at least temporarily, eclipse or transform the calculations and the valuations of pure reason. The insights of *mania* will be reached not by the measuring, counting, and calculating of the *logistikon,* but by nondiscursive processes less perfectly transparent to the agent's awareness, and apparently more difficult for her to control. She is led to action on the basis of feeling and response. It seems likely that her antecedent thinking will not have the logical form of rational deliberation, and, furthermore, that she may be unable to produce, after the fact, a certain sort of rational justification for her action. A "rational" justification would presumably be one that subsumed the action under certain general principles of conduct and pointed to processes of deliberative weighing and measuring that would show us how the choice contributes to some end or ends better than other available alternatives. A good example of the erotic madman, by contrast, might be the Alcibiades of the *Symposium*, whose account of his actions takes the form of a disorderly story concerned with particulars, packed with expressions of and appeals to feeling and emotion. We can discern in it no general principles, no general device of measurement.[15]

It is clear that the pre-*Phaedrus* dialogues do, overwhelmingly, attack *mania* as a "simple evil," a state of the person that cannot lead to genuine insight, and one that, more often than not, produces bad actions. *Mania* is called a species of viciousness at *Republic* 400b2 (cf. Meno 91c3, *Rep.* 382c8). In a number of passages it is linked with excessive appetite-gratification, or *hubris* (*Rep.* 400b2, 403; *Crat.* 404a4). It is linked with delusion, folly, and the "death" of true opinion in *Rep.* 539c5, 573ab (cf. 382e2, *Tim.* 86b4, and Ps-Pl. *Def.* 416a22). And, moreover, it is unequivocally the view of the *Republic* that *any* state in which the irrational dominates will be, no matter what we call it, characterized by the defects of *mania*—the loss of true insight and the tendency to excess. The passage in Book 9 that discusses dreaming tells us that when the *logistikon* is lulled to sleep, the "bestial" elements will take over and attempt to satisfy their "own instincts," "released and let off from all shame and good sense" (571c). Dreams can bring truth *only* if the dreamer can contrive to have them be the work of the rational part alone. Before sleep, he must lull the other parts so that they "may not disturb the better part by pleasure and pain, but may suffer that in isolated purity to examine and reach out toward, and apprehend some of the things unknown to it, past, present, or future" (571d–572b; cf. *Phd.* 65a–d).

This denial of cognitive value to the irrational elements is what we might expect, given Plato's general view of the appetites in this work. The fourth book, in an obscure passage whose general import is, nonetheless, fairly clear, attacks the view that all desires of a human agent, including appetitive desires, are desires for the good, or for their objects *qua* good things. The appetites, including the erotic appetite, are claimed to be brute, irrational forces that simply reach out, each for a particular object.[16] They do not discriminate between drink that is good for me on the whole and drink that is not good for me (438a–439b). Nor are they responsive to the direction of rational judgment, short of actual suppression. Finally, they are by nature insatiable (cf. esp. 442ab). In the absence of direct suppression, they will tend by nature to grow, and to reach out for ever greater amounts of their objects; this is bound to lead to action that is unhealthy for me and injurious to others. Clearly such unteachable forces can never be indices of the good.[17] The emotions fare a bit better: They are conceded to be to some degree responsive to education, and can actually provide reason with valuable support.[18] But without the active and continual direction of reason they, too, will deviate from the good and tend toward violence. This Plato makes clear with his images of the dog (Book 2) and the lion (Book 9), animals that, though capable of obeying orders, are always potentially dangerous, and can never be autonomous, much less give guidance to their masters.

The first two speeches of the *Phaedrus* operate with the *Republic's* simple dichotomy between good sense and madness, rationally controlled and uncontrolled states. The speech of Lysias contrasts the irrational state of the lover with the *sōphrosunē* of the nonlover: Lovers, being "sick (*nosein*) rather than self-possessed (*sōphronein*), reason badly, and cannot control themselves" (231d). Lysias, by contrast, is "not overthrown by love, but in control of myself" (233c); he acts not under passional compulsion, but willingly (231a). The more careful analysis of Socrates' first speech makes it clear that what is in question here is a view similar to the asceticism of the *Republic* and *Phaedo*. There are two ruling principles in a man: "innate appetite for pleasures" and "acquired opinion about the good." The state of the person in which rational opinion about the good is in control is called *sōprosunē*. The state in which the irrational appetite that draws us toward pleasure is in control is called, simply, *hubris* (237d–238a). *Hubris* is said to be "many-named—for it is many-limbed and many-parted" (238a). (We are reminded of the "many-headed beast" of *Republic* 9.) When the appetite for food is in control, that is gluttony; when the appetite for drink is in control, drunkenness. *Erōs* is finally defined as the state in which the irrational appetite for the enjoyment of bodily beauty has gained control over right opinion. Accordingly, in the rest of the speech, the lover is treated as a "sick" person in the grip of "a mindless ruling principle" (241a8), "mindless out of necessity" (241b7). The ex-lover has "gotten insight (*nous*) and self-possession (*sōphrosunē*) in place of *erōs* and *mania*" (241a). He feels nothing but shame about his former actions.

We can see that this speech succinctly reproduces four central claims of the *Republic* concerning madness and the irrational elements:

1. The appetites are blind animal forces reaching out each for a particular object—for example, food, drink, sex—without either incorporating or being responsive to judgment about the good.[19]

2. The appetites, when in control, tend naturally to excess. (Any irrationally ruled state deserves the name of *hubris*.)

3. Because of (1) and (2), the irrational parts can never, even in a well-trained person, function as cognitive elements directing the person toward the good.

4. The rational element is a leading principle both necessary and sufficient for the apprehension of truth and for right choices. It works better the freer it is from the influence of the other elements.

The moral advice of Socrates' first speech is, roughly, the advice of the *Republic:* Cultivate in yourself the state of self-control, and develop the purity of your reason by suppressing the bestial, irrational elements. Form friendships only with people who are similarly self-possessed. (Lysias' speech adds the advice to give yourself sexually to the self-possessed person. This advice, which is, of course, not in keeping with the views of the *Republic,* is omitted, conspicuously and significantly, from the Socratic speech. The omission, arbitrary if Socrates is merely play acting, makes good sense on our hypothesis.) It is somewhat surprising that these two speeches should have been so roundly denounced, often by critics who examine sympathetically the earlier dialogues' account of the desires. Hackforth, dismissing Lysias' speech, speaks harshly of the "cold, prudential calculation" of the speaker, his obliviousness to "romantic sentiment."[20] But Plato has seriously argued elsewhere that we should avoid romantic sentiment, cultivating the cold separateness of the calculating and measuring part. If we grant him the four essential points about the irrational, this moral advice seems sensible and healthy.

B. MADNESS DEFENDED

The *Phaedrus* defense of *mania* is preceded by a recantation. The *daimonion* of Socrates has urged him to "purify" himself in atonement for his speech, which was both naïve and blasphemous. "If *erōs* is a god or a divine being, as indeed he is, he cannot be something bad; but these two speeches spoke of him as if he were bad. In this way they missed the mark concerning *erōs*" (242e). The formal recantation *via* the Palinode of Stesichorus is preceded, then, by a claim about *erōs* that is in direct opposition to the arguments of the *Symposium,* which made a great point of denying its divinity.[21]

And we now notice, as we consider the larger design of the dialogue; yet another way in which it revises the world of the *Symposium.* Stesichorus had told the story, believed by everyone, according to which Helen was seduced by Paris and went off adulterously to Troy, causing trouble for everyone. In the Palinode he apologizes to Helen by creating a myth about her, a story that says that all during the war she was living peacefully and piously in Egypt. We now notice that the *Phaedrus* as a whole has the form of this Palinode. It has long been observed that a number of internal indications require us to place the dialogue's dramatic date between 411 and 404.[22] But an inscription discovered in this century now shows us that there is a problem about doing this. Phaedrus Murrinousios, this very Phaedrus, was implicated, along with Alcibiades, in the impious mutilation of the Herms, and was forced to go into exile from the city between the years 415 and 404.[23] It is thus historically impossible that Phaedrus should really have been in Athens during this time.

We might, of course, take refuge in saying that Plato does not care for consistency, that the setting is some impossible fairytale mélange.[24] But there is another possibility. We might, in the light of the inscription, see the *Phaedrus* as Plato's own Egypt legend. That story wasn't true. You did not get led into disorder and impiety through your appetitive passions, your devotion to *erōs* and to wine. You did not have to go into exile. All the time, in spite of appearances, here you were at Athens, living a good and orderly life, *and* living such a life without ceasing to be an erotic man. *Erōs* is not the simple evil, the simple cause of disorder and impiety, that we took it to be when we wrote about Alcibiades in the *Symposium*.

"This story isn't true," of course, in the literal historical sense. Whether or not the charges were just, Alcibiades and Phaedrus *were* both forced into exile, and the *Phaedrus* is to that extent a fiction. Probably Stesichorus also continued to believe, as his contemporaries did, in the literal historical truth of the Trojan War story. But Plato's Phaedrus legend and Stesichorus' Egypt legend attack the deep moral that has been drawn from the stories of Helen and Alcibiades. They claim that, although perhaps historically false, their stories express a deeper truth about *erōs*—that it can be a constituent of an orderly and pious life dedicated to understanding of the good.

Socrates now begins his second speech, with covered head. Madness, he declares, is not, as we had said, a simple evil. The two speeches [25] had operated with a simple dichotomy between *mania* and *sōphrosunē*, treating the former as entirely a bad thing, the latter as entirely good (244a). But, in fact, neither of these claims is correct. Some kinds of madness can be responsible for "the greatest of goods for us" (244a); and, in some circumstances, self-possession can result in narrowness of vision. An irrationally inspired prophetess can accomplish much good for the country, a self-possessed one "little or nothing" (244b). The inspired kind of divination is "more perfect and more honorable" than the divination "of reasonable men" (*tōn emphronōn*), which works "through reasoning" (*ek dianoias*) (244c). Similarly, the poet who is truly possessed can teach posterity, while the poet who works by rational *technē* alone is "imperfect" and comes to nothing. Finally, Socrates applies these observations to the case of *erōs*: The "transported" (*kekinēmenos*) friend should be preferred to the self-possessed (*sōphrōn*, 245b). What follows will be, it is said, a "proof" of the truth of these claims.

There is little doubt that something new is here. Certain states of irrational possession are said to be both helpful and honorable, even the sources of the "greatest good." The thoroughly self-possessed man, who subdues emotion and feeling to craft, will neither aid his city much through prophecy, nor achieve honor and fame as a poetic teacher, nor be the best sort of *philos*.[26] The moral theorist cannot afford to make sharp and simplistic divisions between bad madness and good *sōphrosunē*. He must examine the cases more closely, divide artfully, and not, in his divisions, "hack off a part in the manner of a bad butcher" (265e). But we must look to the philosophical/poetic "proof" that follows to find out exactly what the value of madness is, and what elements of the received view are being recanted. Three points emerge above all.

1. *The irrational elements are necessary sources of motivational energy.* The image of the tripartite soul in the mythic account likens a man to a charioteer with two horses. Since the charioteer is clearly meant to be the directing, reasoning *logistikon,* we are invited by the image to consider that reason alone, is a relatively impotent moving force. It is not, like Hume's reason, a purely calculative element with no role in selecting ends and goals. On the contrary, one of its major functions appears to be that of valuing and selecting.[27] But we are still asked to see that, as we are, we require the cooperative engagement of the irrational elements in order to get where our reason wants us to go. If we starve and suppress emotions and appetites, it may be at the cost of so weakening the entire personality that it will be unable to act decisively; perhaps it will cease to act altogether. The idea of "nourishing" the irrational plays an important part in Plato's myth. Even divine beings have horses, and even these horses need their food (247e). And the "food of opinion" (*trophē doxastē,* 248b), though perhaps less fine than the food of the gods, is both the best we can get for our horses and a necessary item in our search for understanding and good life. We suspect that we have here a reference to poetry. Poetry is, along with love, a major source of *trophē doxastē* for the soul's irrational elements. This was why the *Republic* cast it out. Here Plato seems to claim that the ascetic plan of the *Republic,* which deprives emotion and sense of the nourishment of close, ongoing attachments, of the family, of dramatic poetry, may result in crippling the personality even while it purifies it. The

starved philosopher may, in his effort to become an undisturbed reason, deprive himself of essential psychic nourishment and block his own search for the good. His case might be like that of a clinical anorexic, who believes she is progressing toward truth and excellence just at the time when she is very near collapse and death. She has to be made to see that the life and health of reason require the intake of nourishment for the body and its function, which appall her.[28] (There lurks in Plato's story a possibility, which the parallel to anorexia makes clear, that lack of nourishment can even produce delusion and sickness in reason itself: The *trophē doxastē,* otherwise a name difficult to comprehend, may be meant to be the food that is required in order to have true *doxa,* even though it is food for the horses; the weak-horsed reason will, in the logic of the story, remain, of necessity, far from the forms, seeing them less, rather than more clearly.)

2. *The irrational elements have an important cognitive role to play in our aspiration toward understanding.* The fact that the continuing good functioning of reason requires the health of the irrational parts would not show that these could or should ever steer or guide reason. But Plato's contrast between madness and *sōphrosunē* is a contrast between irrational-ruled and reason-ruled states. He is clearly claiming that certain sorts of essential insights come to man only through the guidance of the irrational. It is not just that the inspired prophet or poet or lover may live and create reasonably well. The claim is that *without* madness the poetic, prophetic, and/or erotic person will not attain to the best or highest sorts of understanding. The story of the growth of the soul's wings shows us what lies behind this claim. The irrational elements have a keen, natural responsiveness to beauty, especially when beauty is presented through the sense of sight. Beauty is, among the valuable things in the world, the "most evident" and the "most lovable" (250de). We apprehend "a very clear ray of it through the clearest of our senses," and this stirs our emotions and appetites, motivating us to undertake its pursuit. Earthly examples of justice and reason, since they do not engage the cognitive appetites and emotions, are harder to discern; they can be grasped only after an initial education in beauty has quickened intellect (250b,d).[29] Sometimes the sight of beauty arouses only a brutish appetite for

intercourse, unconnected with deeper feeling (250e). But in people of good nature and training, the sensual and appetitive response is linked with, and arouses, complicated emotions of fear, awe, and respect, which themselves develop and educate the personality as a whole, making it both more discriminating and more receptive. We advance toward recollection and understanding by attending to and pursuing our complex bodily/appetitive/emotional responses to the beautiful: The beautiful would not have been readily accessible to reason alone. The state of the lover who has fallen in love with someone good and beautiful is a state of irrational inspiration and possession, in which all elements of the personality are at the same time in a state of tremendous excitement, and in which sense and emotion seem to be guides toward the good and indices of its presence:

> But when one who is fresh from the mystery, and saw much of the vision, beholds a godlike face or bodily form that truly expresses beauty, first there comes upon him a shuddering and a measure of that awe which the vision inspired, and then reverence as at the sight of a god: and but for fear of being deemed a very madman he would offer sacrifice to his beloved, as to a holy image of deity. Next, with the passing of the shudder, a strange sweating and fever seizes him: for by reason of the stream of beauty entering in through his eyes there comes a warmth, whereby his soul's plumage is fostered; and with that warmth the roots of the wings are melted, which for long had been so hardened and closed up that nothing could grow. . . . Meanwhile [the soul] throbs with ferment in every part, and even as a teething child feels an aching and pain in its gums when a tooth has just come through, so does the soul of him who is beginning to grow his wings feel a ferment and a painful irritation. Wherefore as she gazes upon the boy's beauty, she admits a flood of particles streaming therefrom—that is why we speak of a 'flood of passion'—whereby she is warmed and fostered; then has she respite from her anguish, and is filled with joy. But when she has been parted from him and becomes parched, the openings of those outlets at which the wings are sprouting dry up likewise and are closed, so that the wing's germ is barred off; and behind its bars, together with the flood aforesaid, it throbs like a fevered pulse and pricks at its proper outlet; and thereat the whole soul round about is stung and goaded into anguish; howbeit she

remembers the beauty of her beloved, and rejoices again. So between joy and anguish she is distraught at being in such strange case, perplexed and frenzied; with madness upon her she can neither sleep by night nor keep still by day, but runs hither and thither, yearning for him in whom beauty dwells, if haply she may behold him. At last she does behold him, and lets the flood pour in upon her, releasing the imprisoned waters; then has she refreshment and respite from her stings and sufferings, and at that moment tastes a pleasure that is sweet beyond compare. [251 a–e, trans. Hackforth]

This moving and extraordinary description of passionate love is obviously the work of the poet from Himera. It takes the same experience described by the earlier two speeches in detached and clinical terms and enters into it, capturing through imagery and emotive language the feel of being in that crazy state. At the same time it shows how the very madness criticized by the other speeches (we even get the reference to the lover's indifference to family and possessions—compare 252a to 231b) can be an important, even a necessary part of moral learning. The stimulus of beauty is necessary for the growth of the wings; in the boy's absence the personality dries up, and reason itself ceases to develop. The pleasure of the soul in the presence of beauty is a reliable indicator of progress toward the form.

In advancing these claims, this narrative corrects in certain particular ways the view of the appetites advanced in earlier dialogues. The erotic appetite is not a blind urge for the replenishment of intercourse and orgasm. It demands not just any contact with an object that would satisfy a physical tension; it is responsive to beauty, and it also serves as our guide concerning where beauty may be found. Even the worst people, the ones who want to "mount" like four-footed beasts, giving themselves over to pleasure" (250e), look for beautiful objects, not ugly ones. Furthermore, in people of good character, appetite is linked with complex emotional responses that help us discover moral beauty and goodness, both in others and in ourselves. When we fall in love, we also are moved by a tenderness and awe for the beautiful other; this emotion gives us new information, both about ourselves and about goodness of action. We realize that certain ways of acting toward the other person are good when and if they meet with the approval of these emotions; we reject certain ways of acting when we sense that they do not accord with felt reverence. For example, these lovers choose not to have intercourse with one another, even though they express their affection regularly in bodily gestures short of this (cf. 255b), because they feel that the imbalance and excess of appetitive excitation involved in intercourse is incompatible with preserving reverence and awe for the other as other. Appetite is curbed by the demands of the emotions that it has awakened. The *Republic* had urged that our only reliable witness was reason; this myth, though not by any means uncritical of appetite, urges us to see that the situation is more complicated than that. Finally, not the least of the lover's learning is learning about the beloved other—a learning he surely could not get outside of the love relationship. Each, through the responses of sense and emotion, comes to understand and honor the divinity of the other person (252d), seeking to know his or her character and soul through and through. This leads, further, to an increased self-understanding, as they "follow up the trace within themselves of the nature of their own god." So, in his state of possession (*enthousiōntes*), the lover learns the beloved's "habits and ways"—and, through these, his own (252e–253a). If we ask what sort of understanding this is, and what sort of *logoi* the lover can give on the basis of it, we may not get a very tidy answer. The lover will, no doubt, be able to tell some general truths about characters of a certain type. But some of his deepest *logoi* of the other may be more like stories. As Alcibiades, asked to speak about *erōs,* tells us some stories about Socrates, so these lovers may also find that they have to become artists and storytellers to tell the truth. And some of their wisdom may not reveal itself in telling the truth at all. It may be more of an intuitive understanding of how to act toward the other person, how to respond, how to teach, how to limit oneself. But Plato shows us that it is insight and understanding nonetheless, and a kind that is of central importance in moral development.[30]

3. *The irrational elements, and the actions inspired by them, are themselves intrinsically valuable components of a good life.* So far, we might believe that Plato has allowed the irrational a more

liberal role only as a necessary source of motivation toward the good. Once intellect has been led by sense toward the norms of beauty and justice, we can cease to rely on madness, and simply contemplate truth. To say that "the highest goods come to us through madness" is not to say that madness, or the actions of the madman, are themselves intrinsically good. But I believe that the *Phaedrus* gives to the irrational not merely an instrumental, but also a component role in the good.

From the beginning of the recantation, this is suggested. The speeches critical of *erōs*, say Socrates, would not be convincing to a listener who was "of noble and gentle character, who was or had ever been in love with another person of similar character" (243c). This person would think the speeches the work "of men brought up among sailors, who had never seen a case of free and generous love" (243e). Even if we think that Plato's aristocratic disdain for the unpropertied classes has led him to speak unfairly of the navy, we can see what he has in mind. The man brought up among sailors is likely to take an instrumental view of love. He will think of it as calming his needs and as yielding positive bodily pleasure. What he will not learn from his experience in this milieu is that love can be a stable and good part of a good life, a life worthy of a man of free and generous character.

The lovers of the *Phaedrus*, unlike the exploitative sailors of Plato's imgination, live their lives with one another, bound to one another by their erotic passion and by their respect for the other's character, their shared interest in teaching and learning (cf. esp. 252c–253e, 255a–f). Each lover seeks a partner who is similar in character and aspirations (252cff). Having found one another, they treat one another with respect for the other's choices (252de), fostering one another's continuing development (253ab), "using no envious spite or ungenerous hostility" toward the other (253b), but genuinely benefiting him for his own sake. (In these and other ways, they look very much like the character friends of Aristotles's *Ethics*.) Plato describes their passionate longing and emotion for one another in a way that stirs us with its beauty and strongly indicates that he finds their madness beautiful and good. It is crucial that the lover be "not one who makes a pretense of passion, but one who is really experiencing it" (255a). All other friends and associates have nothing to offer, Socrates tells us, in comparison to the inspired friend (255b). *Erōs* is now not just a *daimōn,* but a god: a thing of intrinsic value and beauty, not just a way station toward the good. The best life involves ongoing intense devotion of one individual to another individual. This life involves shared rational activities, but it also involves continued madness, and shared appetitive and emotional feeling. The best lovers stop short of intercourse; but this, as we have said, is only because they feel that in intercourse they are bound to forfeit other valuable irrational elements of their relationship, the feelings of tenderness, respect, and awe. Certainly they are encouraged in any sensuous exploration of the other that stops short of what is seen—not all that implausibly—as an act involving the total surrender of judgment, and therefore as potentially selfish and/or violent.[31]

The lover of the *Symposium* also began by loving a single individual. But he or she soon moved on to a more general appreciation of beauty and relaxed his or her intense love for the one. The pairs of lovers in the *Phaedrus* never do this. Their search for understanding and goodness is accomplished, throughout life, in the context of an intense particular relationship with an individual whose distinctive character is nourished and explored within the relationship. Nothing the lover learns about the good and beautiful ever makes him denigrate or avoid this unique relationship or cast aspersions on anything about it. We do not move on from poetry to philosophy, from bodies to souls to sciences. We never even consider any of these small, or despise them. We remain makers of images, and "boy-lover[s] with philosophy." The good is grasped not by transcending erotic madness, but inside a mad life.[32] Unlike the life of the ascending person in the *Symposium,* this life is unstable, prey to conflict. The lovers have continually to struggle against inappropriate inclinations, to expend psychic effort in order to hit on what is appropriate. Unlike the ascending person, they risk, in the exclusivity of their attachment, the deep grief of departure, alteration, or, inevitably, death. But Plato appears to believe that a life that lacks their irrational devotion—whether or not it had this at some former time—is lacking in beauty and value next to theirs. Socrates concludes, "Such and so many, my child, are the divine gifts that the friendship of a lover will bring you. But the acquaintance of the nonlover, mixed with mortal self-posses-sion *(sōphrosunē thnētē)*, dispensing its mortal and niggardly benefits, giving birth in the beloved soul to a stinginess *(aneleuthe-ria)* that is praised by the many as virtue, will render it devoid of understanding *(anous)* and cause it to roll around and beneath the earth for nine thousand years" (256e–257a). And this blame is not restricted to the *bad* nonlover, or even to the nonlover who has at no former time been a lover. *All* lives bereft of madness and the influence of the other's madness are alike condemned as drab and ungenerous, lacking in the value of insight.

If we now return to the four points in Plato's indictment of the irrational, we find that Plato has recanted or seriously qualified all of them:

1. The appetites are blind animal forces reaching out for an unqualified object. This has been questioned at least for the erotic appetite, which, even in its most degenerate form, seems to be responsive to beauty. Phaedrus and Socrates both remain critical of many bodily pleasures (cf. 258e). It is not denied that *some* of our appetites conform to the *Republic* picture. What is claimed is that that picture was too simple, and, in particular, that it did not tell the whole truth about *erōs*.

2. The appetites tend naturally to excess when not suppressed. Plato still seems to believe that the unruly horse needs constant reining in; it is called a "companion of *hubris*" (253e). But he also seems to believe that this horse should be well fed, and that, properly controlled, it can play a good and a necessary role in motivating the person, even in teaching the person about the beautiful.

3. The irrational elements *cannot* function cognitively. Here, as we have argued, they can and do. A major development is Plato's lengthy and detailed account of the motivating and cognitive role of certain complicated emotions, and his picture of the interaction of sense, emotion, and judgment in *erōs*, which the *Republic* had treated as simply a bodily appetite.

4. The rational element is both necessary and sufficient for the

apprehension of truth and for right choices. Here it is not. Alone it will lead the niggardly life of *sōphrosunē thnētē*. And it is not even, in every particular case, necessary for right choice. In a well-trained person emotional reaction will probably often be sufficient.

But if the old opposition between the rational and irrational has been undercut, the old opposition between poetry and philosophy, the literary and the analytical, must undergo a parallel re-examination. The task of the philosopher, which is the education of the soul toward understanding, can and even must be performed by speech that calls upon the soul's erotic nature and its responsiveness to beauty. Plato's choice of a way of writing that moves back and forth between spare formal argument and the most emotional and emotive outpourings of prose-poetic lyricism indicates to us what he now thinks moral learning requires. The "mortal self-possession" of argument without likenesses and stories will, in its stinginess (a stinginess that many think a virtue), leave our souls devoid of understanding, rolling about beneath the earth.

C. The Person as a Madman

We can use these observations to approach what has long been a hotly contested problem in *Phaedrus* interpretation: What do we make of the fact that this dialogue seems to make use of a conception of the person different from that of the *Phaedo* and the *Republic*? The *Republic* tells me that what I really am is an immortal, rational soul, only contingently associated with a body. The conflicts that give rise to what are called parts of the soul all arise from the soul's union with body; and the conflict-free rational element, the only one that is immortal, is sufficient to preserve my identity outside of the body. The *Phaedo*, using a similar picture, urges me to dissociate myself from my bodily nature and use my life as a practice for separation. Socrates is convinced that everything that goes to make him Socrates will depart from the body at death. His conception of the person makes the body and its needs and desires no part of his identity.[33]

In the *Phaedrus,* as is well known, all souls are tripartite, even the souls of the immortal gods. The proof of immortality does not depend on a premise of noncomposition, as in the *Phaedo,* but only on the self-moving nature of soul. In later dialogues, such things as appetites, hopes, fears, and pleasures are all classified as motions of soul.[34] I think we cannot gloss over this problem by saying that the tripartite gods are just part of the myth.[35] Human beings are tripartite too, before as well as after incarnation; *Phaedo/Republic* souls are not. And the list of soul motions in later dialogues gives clear evidence of a change.

But this should not surprise us by now. The image of the soul is an image of what I value in myself, what I consider to be a part of my identity. The dualism of the *Phaedo* is dependent on that dialogue's moral theory, rather than the other way around. A way of expressing my repudiation of the body and its troublesome desires is to say that that is not really me, not what I really, in my true nature, am. The *Republic*'s myth of Er, which makes my soul out to be a pure, noncomposite rational thing, albeit crusted over by barnacles and other remnants of my earthly existence, is an image of a view about the appetites and reason that has been carefully defended in that dialogue with arguments that start not from a dualistic metaphysics, but only from our exprience of psychological conflict. Since the *Phaedrus* argues against these arguments and this view of the irrational, we should expect it to adopt a new image of the person. It is a question of what I will allow to count as part of me. And in this respect the agent of the *Phaedrus* is tolerant, and generous with his acknowledgments. The radiant vision of the Myth of Er, a myth that is meant to save,[36] is laid aside in favor of Socrates' open question: Am I a being more complex and puffed up than Typho, or rather some tamer and simpler creature? (230a). And later on this question itself is implicitly rejected as still too much in the grip of the *Republic*'s simple affirmations and denials: You can be complex without being Typho, orderly without being simple, a lover without being Alcibiades, a philosopher without abandoning poetry.

III. THE METAPHYSICS OF MORALS

The moral view of the *Phaedrus* looks like a view grounded in a study of the facts of our contingent human nature as we find it in the world, a view that makes not only the instruments of goodness but also the good itself relative to the needs and the beliefs of a particular kind of living being. It thus appears to share Aristotle's metaethics, as well as so much in his view of friendship and the good: What we are after is the human good, and to wish for a good that can only be good for some other sort of creature—say, a god—is not to wish for your good, since it implies a wish that you cease to exist.[37] Aristotle's target in these and related remarks is, presumably, the moral theory of Plato's middle dialogues, which attempts to hold up godlike perfection as a goal for human beings. The *Republic* rejected a method of moral inquiry that made the human, an imperfect being, the measure of truth concerning the good. Once the interlocutors catch a glimpse of the "longer route" to insight through dialectic and the ascent to the Form of the Good, they realize that their previous attempts, which took a human agreement as a measure, were for this reason inadequate. "Nothing imperfect," says Socrates, "is ever the measure of anything" (504c). The only real test of an ethical theory would be its correspondence to the extrahuman and eternal reality of the forms. The forms are what they are independently of the way they appear to any desiring, acting being. Moral truth is stable, pure, nonrelative. In order to attain to it, the philosopher must get rid of the limitations of her merely human nature, learning to think and see like a being that is, itself, maximally stable, self-sufficient, unconstrained. Philosophers try, through education, to "feed" the part of themselves that is most similar to the forms, and to diminish the power of the parts that are needy, variable, reason-upsetting. This means that they can accept into the guardians' curriculum only those stories that deal with stable and pure natures, either human or divine.

There appears, then, to be a deep connection between Plato's realist conception of truth and his denigration both of our irrational nature and of the poetry that deals with it. If the moral truth is something that is "out there," not perspectival, not relative to the needs and interpretations of a contingent and limited being, then it looks as if the best point of view from which to get at it is the point of view of the unlimited and stable god, whose perceptions are not colored by interest or need. To say of something that it is a human interpretation of the world, or a setting down of the human "appearances," is to contrast it, implicitly, with the pure, uninterpreted *logos* of what really is.

The *Phaedrus,* as we see, is more tolerant of the method that looks at the world through human eyes, including eyes that are inspired by madness. It frankly confesses, without perturbation, that the heart of its account of the good is a human likeness, possibly quite different from what a divine intellect might tell (246a). I want now to suggest that a great deal of the moral material we have been discussing can be best understood by connecting it with what seems, in this dialogue, to be a major development in Plato's epistemology: The divine truth, the full, perfect, non-perspectival understanding of the forms that the *Republic* held up as the goal of the philosopher, is now held to be a goal that no human being can ever reach. Socrates contrasts the "divine exposition," which would tell "how it is" with the soul, to his "human and lesser" exposition, which presents a likeness (246a). We are told that only the god-souls have a full and complete view of all the forms in the circuit, as they stand on the rim of the universe. Only their reason is said to see the form of *epistēmē*: "not the *epistēmē* that has change as its attribute, not the sort that is always different in the different subjects that are now called beings, but the real one that really is in a subject that is" (247de).[38] Only they are said to be nourished by "intellect and unblemished understanding" (247d), although this is clearly the "appropriate" food for all rational souls.[39] The account of the gods' vision ends with a strong contrast: "And that, on the one hand *(men),* is the gods' life: but the other souls *(hai d'allai psuchai,* 248a) . . ." We are told that all other souls follow with difficulty, held back by the nature of their horses. Although the best souls do get their heads above the rim, they experience so much trouble that their vision is disturbed. "They scarcely discern the things that are" (248a5). The Greek here is ambiguous, permitting either the interpretation that they succeed in getting a full view, though with difficulty, or the interpretation that they get only a very restricted and blurred sort of view; but later evidence clinches the case in favor of the latter interpretation,[40] for "all" are said to return "imperfect *(ateleis)* in the contemplation of being," and all are fed with the "food of opinion," instead of the nectar and ambrosia of the gods (248b).[41] Furthermore, to be incarnated in a human form it is not even necessary to have been one of the ones peeking steadily over the rim; it is necessary only to have been one who saw at least "something" of the forms (248c)—one, at least, among those who "saw some forms and not others" (248ab). The future philosopher is the one "who saw the most" (*pleista,* 248d), therefore probably one of the rim-lookers. But this "most," this fact that his superiority to the others is one of degree only—he is never said to have seen *all,* or to have seen *fully*—reinforces the lesson of the preceding section. No human soul has had the full divine vision; all are nourished with opinion, rather than with reason's purest and most appropriate food.[42]

But recollection, though it evidently can reach back farther than a single cycle, cannot recover for us what our nondivine souls have never seen or known. Thus, though the mechanism of recollection connects this dialogue to the *Phaedo,* the possibilities and hopes of recollection are more restricted. Our "memory" of the pre-incarnation state is a memory of purity and joy, of initiation into blessed cognitive mysteries (250bc). But the mere glimpse of the forms (or of some forms only) is a dazzling prospect enough to one whose present state feels the heavy weight of "forgetfulness" and "badness" (248c). It seems inevitable that, however well we recover our vision, our understanding of divine things will remain, at its best, "imperfect." The best lovers become "light," "winged," possessed of the greatest good "that human self-possession and divine madness can provide to a human being" (256b). If they manage to live three consecutive philosophical lives, they can take wing and "depart," avoiding afterlife judgment and punishment, perhaps even escaping incarnation forever. But nowhere is this thought to be sufficient to take them across the gap that separates all other souls from the gods. Our understanding is bounded, incurably.

In fact, we are even told that our very ideas of the divine life and the divine intellect are themselves human fictions, based on the experience of a being confined within the limits of a human way of life:

"Immortal" is something said without any reasoned argument
(logos) at all. Without seeing or sufficiently apprehending, we
make up *(plattomen)* a god, a kind of immortal living being
athanaton ti zōion) having a soul and having a body, these being
grown together for all time [246cd].

This speech is both open about the limits to be attached to human
understanding and, at the same time, apparently cheerful about
operating within these limits. We speak only of what we have, as
humans, seen and thought. We make up gods that look like us. But
this Xenophanean insight is not allowed to give rise to a Xenophanean pessimism, or to the *Republic*'s heroic attempt to transcend
the anthropocentric. The poetic fictions embodied in Socrates'
speech are allowed to stand at the heart of the dialogue. We are
supposed to accept them, and to believe them capable of yielding
genuine, life-guiding understanding.

Furthermore, when we reach the part of the dialogue in which
questions of method and of understanding are most extensively
discussed, we find a major new development: the method of division. It is well known that the *Phaedrus,* by introducing the
method that will dominate the later dialogues *(Sophist, Statesman,
Philebus),* breaks new ground in Plato's metaphysics. What has
not been seriously attempted so far is to establish connections of
an interesting kind between the introduction of division and the
moral theory of the dialogues in which division appears. Most
often, dialogues such as *Phaedrus* and *Philebus* are studied piece-
meal; sometimes they are explicitly argued to be piecework, with
little internal unity. But there are connections to be made in the
Phaedrus at any rate, as our preliminary observations might already suggest.

The method of division is a method of analyzing and classifying
our conceptions.[44] It is linked with the "What is it?" question, and
it offers us a way of seeking answers to that question in a wide
variety of cases. We take an analysandum—let us say, Socrates.
We ask, "What is it?" And we note that we can give answers that
bring this particular under sortals of many different kinds: "a philosopher," "a human," "a Greek," "a pale human," "an animal."
The job of division seems to be to draw a map of these answers,

separating the genuine classifying sortals from merely verbal divisions that do not reveal natures of things, and arranging the genuine sortals into a branching hierarchy. (Once we had this sort of answer, we would also be in a position to collect under the basic sortal "human" the other particulars for which this substance sortal supplies criteria of unity, distinctness, and identity. Or, alternately, we might begin with such a "collection" of the particulars.[45] If we perform this sort of conceptual "mapping" properly, we will not include bogus unities such as "foreigner,"[46] hacking off limbs like a bad butcher (265e); and we will not leave out any relevant layers in the hierarchy—as, for example, Philebus does when he thinks he can go from big generic claims about Pleasure directly to particular judgments, without doing the careful taxonomical work that occupies Socrates and Protarchus through the middle section of that dialogue.

The method, as I have roughly described it, has obvious affinities with Aristotelian inquiries into the *endoxa* or *phainomena*.[47] Like Aristotle's careful analyses and classifications, the method seems to concern itself with the interpretations of the world embodied in human language and the human practices of individuating and identifying. Although not every verbal division gives rise to a genuine metaphysical division, the corrective procedures themselves are appeals to what, more comprehensively, we say and do, how we see things. There is in the method—as Gilbert Ryle has noticed[48]—an irreducible "empirical" element: that is, it appears to be inseparable from the linguistic and interpretive practices of contingent mortal beings, their ways of structuring the world.

And yet Socrates speaks of this method with the highest enthusiasm. "I am, Phaedrus, a passionate lover *(erastēs)* of these division and collections, so that I may be able to speak and to think" (266b, cf. *Phlb.* 16b). It is a gift from the gods, which gives us the power "to examine and learn and teach one another" (*Phlb.* 16e). It is repeatedly identified with genuine dialectic (*Phlb.* 17a, *Phdr.* 266bc, *Soph.* 253ce, *Plt.* 285–87); it is, clearly, *the* method of the philosopher. In the middle-period dialogues, the possibility of thought and discourse was pinned on the separate, stable, eternal existence of the Forms, and on our ability to apprehend and give an adequate *logos* of these (cf. esp. *Parm.* 135bc). The method of the philosopher was, in the *Republic,* a method that worked up the ladder of ever more inclusive hypotheses, culminating in the grasping of an entirely unhypothetical starting point, a basis for understanding that is what it is independently of all human theory. From this point, Socrates there announced, demonstration can proceed without in any way relying on the empirical (511bc). The method of division, by contrast, has no unhypothetical points, no nonempirical basis, and no stable or unrevisable elements. The highest genera are arrived at by a collection based on experience, and are judged by their ability to embrace and order that experience. If a new consideration dictates, the hierarchy can be revised even at the very top (cf. esp. *Sophist* 226). The godlike philosopher is now not the one who can give accounts of transcendent and stable forms, but one who can practice supremely well and seriously a method that, in one way or another, is the method on which our ordinary speech itself implicitly relies. He is distinct from the sophist not so much in his subject matter (as Aristotle says) as in his "choice of a way of life" (*Metaph.* 1004ᵇ24–25): his honesty, his seriousness, his dedicated pursuit of understanding.

A metaphysics of morals based on the idea of articulating the "appearances" might be expected to yield a less revisionary ethical theory than the strongly realist metaphysics of the middle-period theory of forms. Our data will be human sayings and beliefs; and, as in Aristotle's method, we seem to be committed to preserving "the greatest number and the most basic" of these. At least we appear to have nowhere else to go. We are never led to expect that division could take us beyond our language and our concepts to a harder or purer truth.[49] We have already been told in the *Phaedrus* that the purer truth is unavailable, except to beings who are, in any case, only our fictions.

Especially in the area of our self-conception, this method seems to yield new and ethically relevant results. The *Republic* philosopher had attempted to conceive of himself, as far as possible, as a godlike intellect, a member of the species Rational, only contingently and *pro tempore* animal. The philosopher of divisions could oppose this method by pointing out the very fundamental place of the sortal concept "man" in our linguistic and other practices: how basic it is in the ways we actually fix criteria of identity, count, classify, individuate particulars. For Aristotle, this metaphysical fact of our human life suggests that an ethical theory cannot simply neglect or banish from the scene anything that we take to be a part of our conception of human identity. To wish a human a life that is no longer a human life is not to wish *him* anything. "A friend wishes his friend good for the friend's own sake—so he will have to remain the sort of creature he is; then he wishes him the greatest good he can have *as a human being*" (*EN* 1159ᵃ5ff).

Such concerns with human identity may lie behind the *Phaedrus*'s connection of division with a newly anthropocentric ethics. Certainly the *Philebus,* another dialogue in which division is prominent, advances moral arguments that look similarly anthropocentric. Consider the following exchange:

SOCRATES: Will such a man be adequately possessed of knowledge, if he can give his account of the divine circle and the divine sphere themselves, but knows nothing of these human spheres and circles of ours, so that, when he is building a house, the rules that he uses, no less than the circles, are of the other sort?

PROTARCHUS: I am moved to mirth, Socrates, by this description we are giving of ourselves confined to divine knowledge.

SOCRATES: What's that? Are we to throw in alongside of our other ingredients the art of the false rule and false circle, with all the lack of fixity and purity it involves?

PROTARCHUS: We must, if we are going to find the way home when we want it.

SOCRATES: And music too, which we said a while ago was so completely dependent on lucky shots and imitation, and so deficient in purity?

PROTARCHUS: I think we are bound to do so, if our life is ever to be a life at all.
[62a–c; trans. Hackforth][51]

The picture of a human being endowed with only divine knowledge now brings a laugh, rather than a thrill of exaltation—because it is being looked at flatly and plainly, from the inside of a human life.

From the remote world of philosophical purity, Protarchus's plain speaking returns us suddenly, with a jolt, to the world we know, where you have an interest in finding your way home and you value things relatively to these interests and practices. It is, I think, significant that it is through this sort of anthropocentric return that poetry is here brought into the good life: We need it if we are going to have a life that counts, for *us* (in terms of our natural desires), as a *life*. Such an appeal to the standing interests of an imperfect being, in justification of a plan for the good, would never have been admitted under the *Republic's* austere interpretation of the proper measure of value. Now *we* are the measure of the world. We can laugh at the idea of a god, with godlike understanding of pure forms, trying to find the road to Larisa, or the entrance to the Lincoln Tunnel. If you live in New York, it might be better to be human.

What could have brought about this shift of perspective—or, rather, this shift to perspective? One suggestion is already lurking in these pages: the influence of Aristotle. But we might also point to one of Plato's own arguments: the paradox of *epistēmē* in the first part of the *Parmenides*. (These two would really be the same suggestion if G. E. L. Owen is right to see Aristotle's hand in the *Parmenides* arguments.)[52] This final paradox raised by Parmenides to trouble the theory of forms is concerned with the notion of unqualified understanding. Parmenides introduces a contrast between "understanding as it is itself" and "understanding among us" or "understanding in our world" *(par'hēmin)*. He gets Socrates to agree that "understanding as it is itself" can have for its object only "the truth in our world" or "the truth among us." And each department of understanding in our world must have as its object some group of truths in our world (134ab). In consequence, the forms as they are themselves, being, by definition, eternal things independent of our human perspective and practices, cannot be grasped as such, in themselves, by human beings.

We might try to elucidate Parmenides' position in the following way. What *we* grasp will be limited by our natures as changing beings in the world. An understanding that is conditioned and limited (that itself "comes to be"), will for this reason be a bounded and limited understanding, grasping truth in a bounded and limited way. We can see truth only *as conditioned* by our ways of seeing. For example, as the *Phaedrus* shows us, we grasp the divine nature in a way that is conditioned by the limitations of an anthropocentric imagination. The unconditioned truth, the truth that is really and eternally true, can be grasped in its fullness only by an unchanging, entirely unconditioned, and stable intelligence, one that does not filter or interpret—so, we imagine, by some god, but never by us. Parmenides is saying that the account of truth in the middle dialogues has been an account of truth-in-itself, not of truth-for-us. Perhaps there is such truth, but it can never be in our world, or be anything to our lives and deliberations. What can be something for us is *human* truth, truth interpreted and shaped by our interests and our constitution. A gap opens up between us and the gods. In the *Parmenides,* that gap is taken, at first, to be a disaster for us. It seems to undermine all our cognitive efforts. (It was a standing danger in Greek epistemology that the anthropocentricity of human rationality would be taken to imply its arbitrariness. So deeply did the opposition nature/convention permeate the tradition that the only way to oppose radical relativism appeared to be the espousal of metaphysical realism; it took heroic effort to show that some of what is man-made may be deep and indispensable, rather than arbitrary and replaceable.) But Socrates goes on, in the wake of the paradoxes, to get some practice in the manipulation of our most basic human concepts. In the dialogue's second part he gains insight, through a kind of "drill" in argumentation, into the logical structure of the human mind: the way, for example, the mind deals with contradiction, the role played by the basic logical principles in human life and thought. He is now ready to practice the method of division. The paradox might have led to speechlessness, and the abandonment of our aspiration to *epistēmē*. It leads instead to our acceptance of a limited epistemic goal and to the adoption of a philosophical method appropriate to advance us towards that human end.

We now see that Socrates' Palinode has yet one more meaning. " 'This story isn't true' " referred, most obviously, to the slanderous story of the earlier speeches (and the earlier dialogues), speeches that, the *Phaedrus* argues, told lies about the relationship between reason and desire. It referred also, playfully, to the fictional status of the myth about Phaedrus, which, itself, corrects a slanderous story that, though historically true, is metaphorically false. But it can now be seen to be, at the same time, a commentary on the *second* speech of Socrates, the speech that introduced itself as a myth and a likeness. Human stories are never true in the way in which the *Republic* demanded the truth: true for no particular species, independently of specific ways of living, true unconditionally and of the unconditioned. And yet the Palinode embraces the pursuit of the human truth, since it goes on to create a myth about the soul that is claimed to embody that truth (cf. *anthrōpinēs*, 246a).

Here poetry enters the argument of the *Phaedrus* once again. We have seen how a changed conception of value, connected with an anthropocentric conception of truth, leads to a greater *tolerance* of the poet. We can now begin to see why these reflections about truth might lead, as well, to a new *need* for poetry. The poet is the person who creates fictions and images freely and exuberantly, a world maker who takes delight in his or her free making. She plays "the game of fiction." She says of her own most serious products, "This story isn't true"—and she says it without fear, or anxiety, or rancor. It does not occur to the poet that the failure of her products to embody literal or unconditioned truth should count against them; that is not what they are trying to do or to be. For this reason, the poet can serve, as happens in the *Phaedrus* with the speech of Socrates-Stesichorus, as a model for the philosopher and the lover, those other creators of truth and value. The philosopher and the lover, those other creators of truth and value. The philosopher has been thrown into perplexity by Parmenides' challenge. He needs to be told that it is all right to practice division; and it is the poet who is best equipped to tell him this. If the philosopher and the lover can be persuaded to accept the anthropocentricity of their enterprise with the poet's "good will to appearance," her acceptance of the conditioned and the human and her resolve to create in the conditioned and the human, the discovery of perspective may bring community and friendship instead of silence and isolation.[53]

But we must now concede that Plato's will toward appearance was never unqualifiedly good. The mood of recantation in the

Phaedrus, its acceptance of limits, and its restoration to goodness of much in our nature that we associate with our finitude are connected, nonetheless, with a deep nostalgia for purity whose expression was never more moving than here. The complexities of the person are given greater respect; but Plato's deep discontent with our bodily nature, his sense that the body is a trap, a shell, are strongly present even in the speech of recantation (esp. 250bc). Disembodiment is a good even for the complex person (whose appetitive soul is taken, oddly to be separable from its bodily vehicle). Images of lightness, loftiness, clarity, and purity are used to characterize the soul's excellence. The person looks to this lightness as to a possible good; and, beyond this, he or she looks, as an impossible dream, to the imagined life of the pure divinities, drinking from the springs of unblemished understanding. Nietzsche, in his lifelong battle with Platonic metaphysics, saw that the acceptance of the human required uprooting altogether the oppositions human/divine and perspectival/unqualified. For the human to be really affirmed, the whole idea of unqualified or pure knowledge had to drop out, even as a wish. Plato, never this pleased with the human, the interpretative, the finite, maintains the oppositions.

But perhaps the practitioner of division cannot do otherwise. For if division is an art of articulating our human beliefs and conceptions, then the refusal of the human and the denial of the body, being among the deepest of the human "appearances," must also have their place. Aristotle ended his "appearance"-saving ethical treatise with Book 10, which, unlike the other books, urges us not to think mortal thoughts, but to "immortalize" as far as we can. It is important to see this not as a violation of the method, but as its faithful completion. Nietzsche saw that getting beyond the "appearance" of refusal required going beyond the human being and the appearances altogether. (He took a love poem of Ovid's, a poem that announces its intention of going beyond the conventional denial of delight in the body, as his motto for this task.)[54] Division, however, is not an art of getting beyond. It is an art of getting clearer about problems, in the company of one's friends.

At the dialogue's end, Socrates prays to Pan and other gods of wild nature, asking for a beautiful inside and an outside that will be a friend of that inside (279bc). The prayer embodies both the dialogue's affirmations and its denials: on the one hand, the reliance on divinities associated with passion, not pure intellect; on the other, the persistence of the distinction without/within, with its possibilities for denigration of the bodily "shell." A wish for the friendship of soul and body is far from being an affirmation of their oneness. But in the dialogue's discovery of the value of a friendship of individuals based on character, complex passion, and mutual well-wishing, Socrates has found a powerful resource toward the continued pursuit of these very questions. He now asks Phaedrus whether "we" need anything more: "For in my opinion the prayer was appropriate" (*metriōs ēuktai,* 279c). This "we," this acceptance of a community of need between interlocutor and teacher, lover and beloved, this genuine respect for the pupil's own view of what he needs, all these are new in Plato's portrait of Socrates. And Phaedrus, "Sparkling," (a role played at readings, Ryle argued, by the young Aristotle) replies, in his turn, with both acknowledged need and good will. "Pray the same for me too. Friends share in everything."

"Let's go," says Socrates.[55]

NOTES

1. This chapter is part of a longer manuscript in progress on practical reason and rational self-sufficiency in Greek ethical thought. It is preceded in that manuscript by chapters on *Republic* and *Symposium,* followed by a long section on Aristotle. (A version of the *Symposium* material is now published as "The Speech of Alcibiades: a Reading of Plato's *Symposium, "Philosophy and Literature* (fall 1979), pp. 131–72). I have written this chapter to include the most immediately pertinent *Republic* material; but, especially in the case of the *Symposium,* whose relationship to this dialogue is complex, I have had to omit a lot that might have been illuminating.

2. R. Hackforth, *Plato's Phaedrus* (Indianapolis: Library of Liberal Arts 1952), p. 37.

3. Hackforth, p. 40. The *Phaedrus* has also been connected with Plato's friendship with Dion—cf. esp. the possible puns on his name at 252el.

4. The *Phaedrus* is now generally agreed to be after the *Republic* in date of composition, probably around the time of the *Theaetetus.* For the arguments and bibliography, see Hackforth, pp. 3–7. On stylometric grounds (avoidance of hiatus), Ritter has placed it just before, but close to, the group *Sophist, Statesman, Philebus, Timaeus* (?—my question mark), *Critias, Laws.* The method of division, apparently introduced here, is found also in *Sophist, Statesman,* and *Philebus.* And

I shall be arguing that Plato's treatment of *epistēmē* reveals an awareness of arguments in the *Parmenides*. These are all strong reasons, quite independent of the dialogue's moral psychology and its alleged recantation of *Republic* views about the poet, for reading it as a transitional piece.

5. *Apol.* 22bc, *Meno* 98b–99c, *Ion* 533e–534b.

6. On the issues involved in rendering Plato's *epistēmē*, in at least some cases, by "understanding" rather than "knowledge," see J. M. E. Moravcsik, "Understanding and Knowledge in Plato's Philosophy," *Neue Hefte für Philosophie* (1978), and M. F. Burnyeat, "Aristotle on Understanding Knowledge," *Aristotle on Science: "The Posterior Analytics,"* ed. E. Berti (Padua: Antenori, 1981). Burnyeat's remarks about *logos* in the last part of the *Theaetetus* are especially pertinent to understanding how the method of division could count as a method for acquiring and presenting *epistēmē*. I have also profited from reading an unpublished manuscript by Jon Moline, "Plato's Theory of Understanding," which contains an interesting discussion of division, and of relationships between this method and the moral theory of the later dialogues.

7. This suggestion would be in accordance with some recent interpretations of *eikasia* in the *Republic's* Divided Line, notably those by John Malcolm, "The Line and the Cave," *Phronesis* 7 (1962), 36–45, and Terence Irwin, *Plato's Moral Theory* (Oxford: 1977), 220–23 and notes. The person of *eikasia* is the one who has not adequately sorted out the appearances, as one might, say, when pressed by the Socratic *elenchos* to produce an account. Thus, though many of his or her beliefs are true, this is a kind of accident, and he or she cannot tell the true from the false. The fact that "we" (*Rep.* 515a) are at the lowest cognitive level with respect to virtue is surely to be connected with the fact that poets are our teachers (see Malcolm, p. 44).

8. On grief and fear, cf. *Rep.* 3, 386aff; 396ab makes explicit the point that the imitation of the bad, even *as* bad, is not permitted. With regard to *erōs*, Plato's view is complicated. In the *Symposium* chapter that precedes, I argue that, in Plato's view, our ordinary attachments to individuals whom we see as unique and irreplaceable are incompatible with virtue and order, and must be transformed.

9. I defend this picture of the ascent in the preceding chapter of my manuscript.

10. Cf. below, pp. 8–10.

11. The *mousikos* may be a poet or a composer of music; usually these occupations would be combined. *Mousikē* is the generic term Plato uses for the poetic-musical education received by young citizens (cf. *Rep.* 376e and 2–3 passim; 52lb, 522ab). It corresponds, as training for the soul, to *gumnastikē* as training for the body. It is, however, unlikely that we are to understand *mousikos* here in the more general sense of "acculturated," "trained." First, the musical *paideia* is clearly not sufficient for leading a high life; but the disjunctive form of 248d suggests that what we want is not merely one of the necessary preconditions of philosophy, but something itself sufficient for goodness. (Below I argue that it is sufficient only because the highest *mousikē* is taken to be a form of philosophy, or not without philosophy). Second, the connection between the philosopher and the Muses is explicitly developed and stressed in the rest of the dialogue (cf. below); it develops that the genuine Muse-lover is not just any culturally trained person, but someone whose life is devoted to the new form of the philosophical art. The contrast between the mere *poiētēs* and the *mousikos* seems to depend on this point. Third, in the *Phaedo* (60e), Socrates' dream that he is being commanded to practice and make *mousikē* never suggests to him the interpretation that he should go on being (as of course he, with his fellow citizens, is) a trained and acculturated person. It suggests to him only two possibilities: that he should go on doing philosophy (which, at first,

he takes to be the "greatest *mousikē*"); and, when that interpretation is doubted, that he should become a poet and put stories into verse (61b). What we are seeing here is that these two interpretations fall together: To practice philosophy is indeed the highest form of *mousikē*, but its proper practice involves the use of *muthoi* and poetic language.

12. Compare *Rep*. 9, 581eff, and *Phd*. 64cff. It is never suggested, in the middle dialogues, that poetry is anything but a very early stage in the future philosopher's education, to be given up for the hypothetical method of dialectic and its pure, nonsensuous deductions. The *Phaedo*, like *Republic* 10, expresses uneasiness about this dismissal of the poet. Socrates, before death, dreams that he should "practice that *mousikē*"—the kind he has despised (cf. above, n. 11). His reference to a need to satisfy a religious demand for purification by returning to poetry (*aphosioumenos*, 60) is echoed, probably deliberately, in the *Phaedrus* recantation scene, as is the remark that the fulfillment of the dream's command requires the making of *muthoi*, not just *logoi* (60d–61c).

13. Plato's use of myth is a complex subject. If one is inclined to see the presence of myth in earlier dialogues as undercutting my contrasts, I would insist, first of all, that the myth of Er embodies a conception of the person quite different from that of the *Phaedrus* (cf. below, pp. pp. 17–18). It is also conspicuous that myth in the *Republic* is merely an appendage to the argument, no essential part of getting it to its conclusions. It reaffirms what *logos* has already told us. The *Phaedrus* myth, on the other hand, presents what *logos* cannot capture, and occupies the heart of the dialogue.

It goes along with this that the *Phaedrus* seems to count as dramatic poetry in a more full-blooded sense than the *Republic*. The characters are more particularly characterized, and have a more fully elaborated setting and situation. They have a close and complex friendship with one another, and both move each other and are moved by speeches. They seem, indeed, to exemplify the highest life of the *Phaedrus*, a life in which erotic elements, even erotic tensions, play an ongoing and a major role.

14. Cf. esp. *Rep*. 403, *Symp*. 213d, *Crat*. 404a4; on the opposition to *sōphrosunē*, see esp. *Protag*. 323b5, *Rep*. 573ab.

15. This point is further developed in my *Symposium* article.

16. See T. Irwin, *Plato's Moral Theory*, 123–24, 191–95, and T. Penner, "Thought and Desire in Plato," in *Plato*, ed. G. Vlastos (Garden City, N.Y.: Doubleday 1971), 96–118.

17. This view of appetite, and its political consequences, are further discussed in my "Shame, Separateness, and Political Unity," in *Essays on Aristotle's Ethics* ed. A. Rorty (Berkeley: University of California Press, 1980).

18. On *thumos* and emotion, see Irwin, 193–95. Plato nowhere gives a systematic story about the differences between this part and the appetitive part, in terms of its relationship to belief and judgment; the *Philebus*, however, does explore these issues in a related and pertinent way. It seems wrong to view the *Republic* division as a simply arbitrary, a result of the antecedent political division.

19. It should, however, be noted that Socrates' first speech connects the erotic appetite with beauty, thus anticipating the view of his second speech. Contrast *Republic* 580e, which mentions only intercourse (*aphrodisia*), and 586ab, which uses animal language of human intercourse. The *Philebus*, presumably after the *Phaedrus*, classifies *erōs* not with the desires for bodily replenishment, but with complex emotions like anger, grief, envy—states grounded in beliefs about the object (47eff). Contrast the different uses of the verb *eran* at *Rep*. 403a, *Phd*. 68a.

20. Hackforth, p. 31.

21. See *Symp*. 198b–204c.
22. See Hackforth, p. 8. Lysias returned from Thurii to Athens in 412–11; Polemarchus, who died in 404, is still alive.
23. Cf. K. J. Dover, "The Date of Plato's *Symposium*," *Phronesis* 10 (1965), 7, n. 15. The relevant inscriptions are *SEG* xiii.13.188, 17.110; cf. B. D. Merritt, *Hesperia* 8 (1939), 69ff, J. Hatzfeld, *REA* 41 (1939), 311ff. Dover points out that Hackforth should have known this information.
24. Cf. L. Robin, *Platon, Phèdre* (Paris: 1939), who calls the scene *"en dehors de toute histoire."*
25. Socrates links the Lysias speech and his own first speech very closely together: Note the duals at 242e–242a.
26. It should be noticed that *philos* and *philia*, not the prominent love words in the *Symposium*, here attain new importance, in keeping with the dialogue's more Aristotelian view of personal relations. The dialogue begins with *ō phile Phaidre*, and its next-to-last line is the proverbial *koina ta tōn philōn*.
27. These concerns are developed at length in my *Republic* section; for a persuasive account of the parts of the soul in these terms, see Gary Watson, "Free Agency," *JPhil* (1975).
28. On the anorexic, see the review of the recent psychological literature in Rosemary Dinnage, "The Starved Self," *New York Review of Books* 26 (1979), 6ff. Aristotle makes related criticisms of Plato's ideal state in vol. 2 of the *Politics:* By removing the family, it weakens and makes "watery" all human ties, diminishing the motivation for public-spirited activity. In the myth of the cicadas that follows his second speech (259bc), Socrates emphasizes the danger that the discovery of an art—including the art of philosophy—will make the artist forgetful of necessary food and drink, even to the point of death.
29. These points receive illuminating discussion in Iris Murdoch, *The Sovereignty of Good* (London: 1979), 59–60, 84–86; unfortunately, her recent *The Fire and the Sun*, a book devoted to Plato's views of art and beauty, does not seem to me to add much to these remarks; see my review in *Philosophy and Literature* 2 (1977–78).
30. These points are more fully discussed in my article on the *Symposium*.
31. See esp. 255b7–8 *(plēsiazēi meta tou haptesthai)*, and the discussion in Gregory Vlastos, "Sex in Platonic Love," Appendix II to "The Individual as Object of Love in Plato," *Platonic Studies* (1973), 38–42.
32. The absence of an ascent to a unitary vision of the good may be connected with the fact that the *Phaedrus* nowhere introduces the form of the good, nor says that the good is something unitary. The forms appear, even by the gods, to be seen one by one, without the sort of overall ordering that the Form of the Good would provide. Perhaps Plato is rethinking more generally the position on the unity of values that underlies the ascent.
33. *Republic* 10 makes it clear that only the noncomposite rational part of the soul is immortal; its arguments could not establish immortality for any other part. We are to see the other "parts of the soul" as arising from the contingent union of soul and body; the view is thus not very different from the *Phaedo's*, which uses only the simpler soul/body dichotomy. On all these points, see W. K. C. Guthrie, "Plato's Views on the Nature of the Soul," in *Plato* [above, n. 16], 230–43.
34. Cf. esp. *Laws* X.896cd.
35. Cf. Guthrie, op. cit.
36. *Rep*. 621bc.
37. Cf. EN 1159ᵃ8ff, 1166ᵃ18ff.

38. This contrast is probably to be connected with the remarks about the instability of "our" *epistēmai* at *Symp.* 207e–208a, where Diotima unequivocally says that *epistēmē* in a changing, growing, and decaying being like the human being is doomed, like that being, to *genesis* and *phthora*.

39. Cf. Hackforth's note on the construction of this passage, p. 78.

40. Cf. Hackforth's translation, "She has much ado to discern *(mogis kathorōsa)* the things that are." "He F's *mogis*" can mean "He succeeds in F-ing, Fs fully or completely, but after some difficulty"; but also, when the achievement admits of degree, it can mean "F's in a constricted or diminished way," "hardly F's." Most occurrences are ambiguous between these, but there are several unambiguous examples of the second in Plato; cf. esp. *Tim.* 50b2, where *mogis piston* means "hardly trustworthy at all," and *Laws* 644, where the interlocutor says, "I can barely follow you *(mogis ephepomai),* but go on as if I were following" (d4); here *mogis* must be taken to deny that successful following has been accomplished. As for *kathoraō*, it can mean "to have within view," "to see distinctly," in which case it is a success verb; but it can also mean "to regard," "to look down upon," "to inspect." A passage very relevant to this present one is Aristotle, *Parts of Animals* 644b30, where he contrasts the "fleeting and partial glimpse" *(mikron morion katidein)* we have of the heavenly bodies with the many things of which we have a fuller and more accurate knowledge *(polla . . . di'akribeias idein).* Here, apparently, *katidein* itself indicates the glancing, partial nature of the vision, as contrasted with *idein.* So the ambiguities of *mogis kathoraō* are multiple, and context must determine what is going on.

41. It is barely possible that the "all" here refers only to those who did not get heads up over the rim. But in this case the story is strangely incomplete: We are never told how the philosophical souls return, or how they are nourished. In what follows, the philosopher is put together with other prehuman souls, and contrasted with them only by the amount or degree of his vision (cf. below and 248d).

42. It should also be noticed that a glimpse of any part of the true forms (*ti tōn alēthōn,* 248c) is sufficient to avoid incarnation until the next cycle. It is only when some soul who, in a previous cycle, saw some of the forms, but on this cycle has failed to do so through "some mischance" *(suntuchia tis)* that filled it with "forgetfulness and vice" (248c), that a human embodied being is produced. The cause of the failure is obscure; the coupling of *lēthē* and *kakia* does not seem to me to allow a decision between cognitive and ethical deficiency. It should also be noticed that this fall may be distinct from the falling of a part of soul that gave rise to the individuation and the embodiment of mortal creatures in the first place (246b7–c6). Prior to that fall (the cause of which is also obscure), there seems to have been a vast reservoir of soul, described only in mass terms, which directed and ruled the whole of the universe. The only story of soul individuation we are given begins with the falling of a part away from the rest. It seems plausible to suppose that recollection can extend back no farther than the moment of individuation: I cannot, as myself, as a unitary soul with a unitary career, recover the state of a part of the ruling soul. If, on the other hand, the two falls are not meant to be distinct, then we must, to fit the earlier to the later story, see the distinction of divine/nondivine as implicit in the story of "all soul," from its beginnings. Though textually harder, this is not impossible, since the mass talk may simply be generalization about a large number of individuals of different types.

43. The discussion of the fitting account of the gods in 2–3 of the *Republic* is in the tradition of Xenophanean de-anthropomorphizing; cf. especially 380d–383c.

44. On the method of division, see J. L. Ackrill, "In Defence of Platonic

Division," in *Ryle,* ed. O. Wood and G. Pitcher (Garden City, NY.: Doubleday 1970), 373–92, and J. M. E. Moravcsik, "The Anatomy of Plato's Divisions," in *Exegesis and Argument,* ed. A. Mourelatos, E. Lee, and R. Rorty (Assen: Von Gorcum 1973), 324–48.

45. This is a highly controversial interpretation of difficult material in the *Philebus,* and I do not want here to press its claim against other candidates. It does not matter very much for my purposes whether the method begins with particulars or with classes; and I suspect it does not particularly matter within the method.

46. See *Statesman,* 262c–263a.

47. See Ackrill, op. cit., 388–90.

48. Cf. Ackrill discussion of passages from *Plato's Progress,* pp. 382–85.

49. Further related points, growing out of the observation that division is a kind of "mapping" of the world, are made by Moline in the unpublished manuscript mentioned above, n. 6; Moline argues for a connection between these metaphysical developments and the more democratic political theory of the *Laws.*

50. The connections between metaphysics and ethics suggested by these remarks are the subject of the Aristotle chapters that follow this in the manuscript described above, n. 1.

51. It is, however, worth noting that this discussion does seem to leave it open that a human being can have "divine knowledge," whatever that is, and give adequate accounts of divine entities. In this respect, the *Philebus* departs less radically from the epistemology of the *Republic* than does the *Phaedrus.*

52. See G. E. L. Owen, "A Proof in the *Peri Ideōn,*" in R. E. Allen, ed., *Studies in Plato's Metaphysics.*

53. Cf. Nietzsche, esp. *Gay Science,* 107.

54. See esp. "How the True World Finally Became a Fable," *Twilight of the Idols,* and, for the Ovid motto, the preface to *Ecce Homo.* Cf. also Stanley Cavell, "Epistemology and Tragedy: A Reading of *Othello,*" *Daedalus* (Summer 1979).

55. I am very grateful to Myles Burnyeat and to Gregory Vlastos for their careful and helpful criticisms of a draft of this chapter; I have also profited from reading an unpublished paper by Burnyeat on the *Phaedrus* theory of recollection. I would also like to thank audiences at the Bodega Bay Conference on Plato's Aesthetics and at the University of Texas at Austin for their comments and questions, and particularly the organizers of the Bodega Bay Conference, Julius Moravcsik and Philip Temko, for arranging a stimulating occasion on which to discuss these issues.

CHAPTER V

Plato and the Poets

James O. Urmson

Our greatest goods come to us through madness, says Socrates in the *Phaedrus,* provided always that it is one of the kinds of madness that are the gift of the gods. One god-given type of madness is that of the poet (*Phaedrus* 244a). Indeed, the poet could be thought of as possessed, as being but the mouthpiece of the Muse herself. Thus the *Iliad* begins with the words: "Sing, goddess, the destructive anger of Achilles the son of Peleus." This must not be thought of as merely a conventional gesture, though it was conventional, any more than Milton's invocation of the heavenly Muse at the beginning of *Paradise Lost* is mere convention:

Of man's first disobedience . . .
Sing, Heavenly Muse, that, on the secret top
Of Oreb, or of Sinai, didst inspire
That shepherd who first taught the chosen seed
In the beginning how the heavens and the earth
Rose out of Chaos. . .

Philosophers are not accustomed either to asking for or to receiving much in the way of divine guidance; but this should not blind them to the fact that many people do ask for it and sincerely believe that they get it. Likewise the Muses spoke to Hesiod on Mount Helicon and made the peasant farmer a poet—the Muses make some men poets as Zeus makes some men kings (*Theogony* 33ff and 94ff.).

Parallel with and not strictly compatible with the idea that the Muse spoke through the poet's mouth was the notion that she inspired the poet. Nowadays we are inclined to think of poetic inspiration as the gift of artistry, of expressive mastery. But that was not the old idea. Milton's heavenly Muse, as the reader will have noticed, was the source of information for the first few chapters of the book of *Genesis,* and is being asked by Milton for more information on the topic; in this Milton was showing himself the accurate classical scholar that he was. In the *Iliad* Homer's first request to the Muse was that she would tell him what caused Achilles and Agamemnon to quarrel, and throughout the *Iliad* he continues to ask the Muses, the daughters of Memory, for factual information: 'For you are goddesses, and are present, and know all things, but we have only hearsay and know nothing' (*Iliad,* Book II, l. 484–85). Similarly in the first two lines of the *Odyssey* Homer asks the Muse to tell the story of Odysseus and makes clear that the need is for solid facts. As reasonably accurately and totally absurdly translated by Pope he pleads with her:

> Oh, snatch some portion of these acts from fate,
> Celestial Muse! and to our world relate.

Plato would not challenge this tradition. Though philosophically an innovator, he was in practical matters a committed conservative. He was trying desperately to shore up the old ways, the old morality, the old patriotism, or what seemed such to his nostalgic eyes. He never wrote anything that could be construed as being inconsistent with or derogatory from the ancient religion of Greece. In the *Laws* he somewhat archaically advocates worship of the sun and the moon, visible gods in a visible heaven. But it is hard to believe that his writings on these matters accurately reflect his own beliefs; it is rather that he thinks that the only religion of which the common herd is capable should be supported by the elite. To this extent he was of like sentiment with Lord Melbourne, who admitted that he was not a pillar of the established church but claimed to be a buttress thereof, since he supported it from the outside. Plato therefore conformed, but in the *Timaeus* he tells us that the maker and father of this world is hard to find and when found is impossible to tell to the masses (28c). In the *Laws* he permits himself to describe the inspiration of the poets as a *palaios muthos* (719c), an ancient myth or tale, but he never denies it and often affirms it. But, in any case, in allowing inspiration to the poets Plato was not committing himself to the view that they always spoke truth. The Muses told Hesiod that they were capable of telling a pack of lies as well as of truth telling. If Plato regarded the poets as inspired, or spoke as though he did, this was in no way incompatible with regarding them as a danger to society. How and why he so regarded them will be the subject of the rest of this chapter.

By the end of the ninth book of the *Republic* Socrates has finished his task of showing that justice is an intrinsic good for those who practice it. At the beginning of the tenth book Socrates looks back over the discussion and says that one of the best things they had done in building the ideal city was to exclude all mimetic poetry from it. He says that the rightness of this decision is now clearer than it had been initially as a result of the subsequent proof of the tripartite nature of the soul. I want to consider what he was rejecting and, second, why he rejected it. I do not propose to argue that Socrates' position is satisfactory nor that it is unsatisfactory. But I do believe that it will emerge that the discussion in the *Republic* is by no means as irrelevant to modern attitudes to imaginative literature as is commonly suggested.

First, then, what is Socrates rejecting? In his own words, literally translated, it is "Poetry, so much of it as is mimetic." Whatever these words may mean, I take it that they do not mean the same as "such parts of mimetic poetry as are undesirable;" he is talking about all mimetic poetry. What, then does he mean by "mimetic"? Since he refers us back to the earlier discussion in book 3, it is a perfectly natural and reasonable expectation that he now means by "mimetic" what he very clearly explained that it meant in book 3. There he tells us that mimetic poetry is to be distinguished from narrative poetry; mimetic poetry is that in which the reciter plays the part of some character and utters what are supposed to be that character's words; it is *oratio recta*, it is direct dramatic representation, it is vocal acting. Narrative poetry is that in which the poet or reciter describes *propria persona* the events portrayed; insofar as speech of others is reported, it is reported in *oratio obliqua*.

But reasonable as the initial presumption is that this will be what he means by "mimesis" in book 10, it is, it seems clear, a quite different position, employing a different conception of mimesis, which is defended in that book. In book 3 Socrates maintains, as a canon of elementary education, that the young should not be permitted to play the part of bad or ridiculous characters—actually to play the part is damaging to the character in a way that narration is not; we may read about Thersites, but not act Thersites. Such is the gist of the argument on Stephanus pages 392 to 398. So, in contrast with the total elimination of mimetic poetry in book 10, not all even of directly dramatic acting is forbidden in book 3, not all of *mimetike,* as there defined, but only a portion of it.

Moreover, it cannot be this notion of *mimesis* that Socrates is employing in book 10, for two reasons. First, Socrates introduces the discussion in book 10 not by saying, as we might expect, that he has already given a perfectly clear account of *mimesis,* but by saying (595c) that he is not at all clear what mimesis is supposed to be; he then gives the famous account of it in terms of the three beds, which affords absolutely no basis whatever for the distinction of drama and narrative made in book 3. If we were to attempt to apply the distinction of book 3 to painting, I suppose that painting a piece of canvas to look like a bed would be narration, and painting oneself to look like a bed would be mimetic. There is no hint in the *Republic* of such absurdities.

Second, as we shall see, the objections to mimetic poetry in book 10 have as much relevance to narrative poetry as to mimetic poetry as defined in book 3. The book 3 distinction is simply irrelevant to book 10. With an amiable desire to make Socrates consistent, such writers as Cross, Woozley, and Tate have held that when he speaks of mimetic poetry in book 10 he really means only bad poetry that is mimetic in the sense of book 3. But not only do all the objections of book 10 apply to narrative as easily as to drama, most of them apply with at least equal force to the portrayal of the good and the beautiful as to the portrayal of the bad and the ugly. In book 3 we were concerned with censorship, the elimination of the morally undesirable—not the elimination of the equivalent of sensational pulp literature, but of the objectionable parts of Homer and other good literature. In modern terms, it is like a prosecution of *Lady Chatterley's Lover* or *The Naked Lunch,* not of cheap pornography. But in book 10 the strictures are intended to apply with equal force to the equivalent of *War and Peace* and *Crime and Punishment.* The complete works of Homer, Aeschylus, Sophocles, and Euripides are to be eliminated. We can represent the argument of book 10 as resuming that of book 3 only by doing gross violence to one or the other or both.

I think that Socrates' basic objection to mimetic poetry as a whole is given on page 595b5. Mimetic poetry is destructive of the intelligence of those of its hearers who do not have the protection of knowing what sort of thing it is—that is to say, who are not philosophers. Nonphilosophers do not know that what is offered by the poet is at two removes from reality. The lover of sights is even unaware that the world of becoming is anything other than the truly real; still less does he realize that what is depicted in mimetic poetry is one grade still farther away from reality. Philosophers are safe from the intellectual corruption of mimetic poetry, as they are from the lures of advertisements of breakfast cereals; but other men are not, and for the sake of the city as a whole, mimesis must go. All mimesis, of good men as of bad men, of heroic deeds as of vice, is a dream of a dream. Most men cannot distinguish dream from reality.

The illustration of the three beds is not designed as an attack on painting; it is a highly stylized illustration to clarify the nature of mimesis. What is said is intended to be directly applicable to mimetic poetry; it includes the following three points:

1. He who understands beds is primarily the user and secondarily the maker of beds. The painter of pictures of beds needs no understanding of beds.

2. The painter of pictures of beds does not attempt to paint beds as they are known to be but the way they look; to do this convincingly is precisely his skill.

3. At a distance a child or a fool may be deceived into taking a picture of a bed for a bed.

How is this highly stylized account of *trompe-l'oeil* painting to be applied to mimetic poetry, Plato's serious prey?

If we were to insist on an overliteral parallelism, the answer would have to be that the poet was trying to reproduce the world of becoming in such a way that not too attentive children and idiots would be deceived into believing that what they were witnessing was some transaction in the world of becoming. They would believe that in the theater they were actually witnessing a quarrel between Creon and Antigone, Oedipus questioning Teiresias, or Medea threatening vengeance. This sort of mistake can indeed be made; there were a number of halfwits in England who sent wreaths to the funeral of a character in a radio serial. But I do not think that Plato was seriously worried about this possibility, any more than by *trompe-l'oeil* painting. I do not even think that he was worried about the falsification of history—after all, in his earlier discussion of falsehood he had suggested that one of its more permissible uses was to fill up gaps in known history (382d).

But Plato does wish seriously to maintain in some sense that the mimetic poet has no need to understand the world of becoming that he depicts, that he does not even attempt to depict the world as it is but only the way that it appears to be—that is his skill—and that people who are not philosophers can be misled into thinking that he gives insight into reality rather than the plausible imitation that in fact he offers. We must try to understand this view in more detail.

In the *Ion* Homer is called the best and divinest poet of all (530b), a view to which Plato without a doubt sincerely assented. Prominent in Homer's alleged merits, however, is the fact that he has "described war for the most part, and the mutual intercourse of men, good and bad, lay and professional and the ways of the gods in their intercourse with each other and with men" (531c). The rhapsode Ion is now represented as taking Homer as an authority on the various themes on which he writes: Ion even claims that as a result of being a specialist on Homer and having an intimate knowledge of Homer's descriptions of strategy he himself is now the best general in Greece: "Be sure of it, Socrates; and that I owe to my study of Homer" (541b). But Socrates points out again that the *techne* of Homer was that of the poet and that as a poet he has no understanding of war or chariot-racing or medicine, though much advice on these topics is given by alleged authorities in his poems.

It should be noted that it is Homer's skill in and understanding of matters other than poetic technique that are being called into question. There is also no suggestion that Plato is worried about possible historical inaccuracies in the Homeric narrative. In the passages on censorship in book 3 Plato criticizes some of Homer's descriptions of the behavior of gods and heroes as blasphemous or inappropriate, not for mere inaccuracy of fact. But in the *Ion*, and, as we shall see, in book 10 of the *Republic*, it is the lack of skill and understanding of the poet overall, not his occasional scurrilities, that is criticized. Certainly Homer and the rest are not being ejected merely on the ground that they are unreliable historians.

The poets' lack of skill and understanding, insisted on in the *Ion*, is harped on again in the *Republic*. Socrates (599) asks what Homer was good at; if he really understood warfare, medicine, chariot-racing, and the like, why was he not a famous practitioner in these areas as well as in poetry? But here, more than in the *Ion*, Socrates emphasizes not merely the poets' lack of the technical skills that they purport to describe; now he argues that the poet as such is not an authority on excellence and evil. Poets are *mimetai eidólon aretes*—imitators of images of excellence (600e5). The poet (602b) will produce his imitations not knowing in each case in what way it is good or bad. Not knowing the reality he will, it seems, imitate what appears fine to the ignorant multitude. The poet's skill in writing (601a) gives his product a charm that makes what he says seem plausible. This lack of understanding of the nature of good and evil, accessible only to the philosopher in Plato's view, is surely the main indictment of mimetic poets.

So the first point by Socrates in book 10 of the *Republic* is one made constantly by him. It is made in so early a dialogue as the *Apology*, where Socrates is represented as saying (21d): "The poets say many fine things, but know nothing of that of which they speak." The poet has only the skill of composition, but is treated as a man with skill and understanding of many things, even of good and evil and the soul of man, an understanding he has not but which he seems to have because of the skill he has in producing a spurious appearance of understanding.

But Socrates now (604) has a further point to make, which I do not recollect that he makes elsewhere; presumably it is this point that becomes clear in the light of the tripartite analysis of the soul. It would be dull to represent a man acting in the face of calamity of the sort that occurs in tragedy as a gentleman of good character would behave. A gentleman hides his grief from the public eye, his anger and his joy are restrained, he does not rant and rail. Homer

represents Achilles exhibiting frenetic grief at the death of Patro-
clus in a way in which a man of good character would be ashamed
to exhibit it. So not only are the poets ignorant of the nature of
moral excellence, they also have a standing temptation to represent people who are supposed to be heroes as behaving in a
theatrical and intemperate manner. In the theater we are led to
admire what outside of it we would despise. The appeal is to the
lowest of the three elements in the soul and we admire characters
whose appetites and emotions are in control of their reason.

We have rehearsed what Plato says. At this stage the expositors
of Plato begin to speak, if friendly, in an apologetic tone and, if less
friendly, with some condescension. Homer, we are told once
again, was the bible of the Greeks; they read him as an authority on
early history, theology, warfare, and the like, and no doubt this
was a mistake. But this, the critics continue, has no relevance to
aesthetic or to literary criticism. Plato simply fails to look at things
from the aesthetic angle. Maybe Homer was no theologian and a
poor strategist—but that is irrelevant to this merits as a poet.
Sometimes the critics appear not to be able to assimilate what they
read, in their horrified incredulity. Thus Nettleship, in his lectures
on the *Republic*, sums up the passage that we have been discussing
as follows: "Rightly or wrongly, Plato has here come to the conclusion that nearly all the imitative art of his time has degenerated into
indiscriminate catering for common excitement. He treats art as
being this and only this, and in consequence the whole passage
remains rather an attack on certain developments of art than an
adequate theoretical treatment of it." Degenerate imitative art of
his time indeed, when all his references are to Homer and the
tragedians! Moreover, Plato is not writing a treatise on aesthetics
but explaining why poetry of an imitative sort must, in spite of its
manifest attractions, be excluded from the ideal state.

I reiterate that I do not want to attack or defend Plato's criticism
of imitative poetry. But I do want to say that, justified or
unjustified, it is just as relevant to modern literary criticism as to
anything in his own day. That is what I now proceed to show.

First let me say again that Plato is attacking mimetic poetry
using as examples those poets whom he clearly believes to be the
best. He has primarily in mind his beloved Homer and the great

tragedians of the fifth century. It is the tragedian who is said (597e6) to be at two removes from reality and the attack is explicitly stated (598d7) to be on tragedy and its leader, Homer. Actual examples are mostly taken from Homer, although (595b9) "a certain love and respect that I have had from childhood makes me hesitate to speak about Homer." Further, it is now the whole of their works that are to be banished.

It is clear who would be the modern equivalent of these great literary figures whom Plato banishes. Certainly the great playwrights, Shakespeare and the rest, must be included. But I have no doubt that the serious novelists may be included also. Plato mentions only poets, but it is not meter that is the target of his criticism. The simple fact is that all fiction in his time and before it was written in verse; there were no prose romances. So let us add Tolstoi, Hardy, Dostoievsky, Henry James, and the rest to our list of the giants of literature whom Plato would expel.

Now, what sort of thing do critics write about these great literary figures and their works? Do they attribute to them the merits that Plato denied them? It would be unwise for me at this stage to offer my own generalizations, so I must ask you to bear with a number of quotations from famous literary critics:

1. "The multitude of things in Homer is wonderful; their splendor, their truth, their force, and variety; he describes the bodies as well as the souls of men." Hazlitt, "On Poetry in General," from *Lectures on the English Poets*

2. "In the first and lowest side of drama . . . I place those pieces in which we are presented with only the visible surface of life. . . . The second place in the scale of dramatic art is due to effective representations of human passions where the deeper shades and springs of action are portrayed. . . . But I conceive that the stage has yet another and loftier aim. Instead of merely describing the enigma of existence, it should also solve it." Friedrich von Schlegel, *Lectures on the History of Literature*

3. "The first and last aim of art is to render intuitively perceptible the process of life itself, to show how the soul of man develops in the atmosphere surrounding him." Hebbel, *Journal* [1838]

4. "It is here [in truth of detail] in very truth that he [the

novelist] competes with life; it is here that he competes with his brother the painter in *his* attempt to render the look of things, the look that conveys the meaning, to catch the color, the relief, the expression, the surface, the substance of the human spectacle." Henry James, *The Art of Fiction*

5. "It [the novel] is an attempt to find . . . in the aspect of matter and in the facts of life what of each is fundamental, what is enduring and essential—their one illuminating and convincing quality—the very truth of their existence." Joseph Conrad, preface to *The Nigger of the Narcissus*

6. "A good poem helps to change the shape and significance of the universe, helps to extend everyone's knowledge of himself and the world around him." Dylan Thomas, *On Poetry*

I cease to quote, not from lack of material but lest I exhaust by iteration the reader's patience. I hope to have given, finely expressed by distinguished writers, specimens of the view that Plato is attacking. All these authors, he would hold, mistake the imitation of a shadow for reality. They are prisoners in the cave and what they take for the deep truths of imaginative literature are in fact shadows on the wall. What a revealing picture of remorse and the craving for expiation Dostoievsky gives us in *Crime and Punishment*, we exclaim. But, Plato asks, why should you think it in any way truthful? It is so utterly convincing, we answer. Indeed, Plato replies, to be convincing is the skill of the writer of fiction, a skill that Dostoievsky has in abundance; but why should we regard the novelist as having any particular insight into the human soul, the criminal mentality, the repentant sinner? To claim such knowledge for Dostoievsky is precisely parallel to the claim that Homer had insight into strategy, medicine, and the virtues and vices of man. It is the philosopher, not the plausible imitator of the world of becoming, who has the insight into good and evil. Such, I think, is the way that Plato would apply his attack to modern literature and the view of it taken by the critics and, no doubt, many lesser readers.

I repeat that it is no part of my design to attack or to defend these views of Plato. The further charge that he would no doubt make, that the great tragic heroes of modern literature, Hamlet, Othello, and the rest, are not heroes but intemperate men whose souls are swayed by appetite, passion, and caprice, I leave also without comment.

What I hope to have established in this chapter is that:

1. Plato is not attacking inferior literature; his attack is on the very best mimetic poets that he knows of, especially Homer, "the best of poets and first of tragedians" (607a).

2. Plato principally attacks them because they give a very convincing show of apparent insight into important matters of which they know nothing.

3. So far from Plato's charges being obsolete, they are directed against a view of serious imaginative literature that is still very common in modern times.

Once again, I say that I offer no comment of my own. But I allow myself the luxury of one further quotation from an author who appears to side neither with Plato nor with those whom I take Plato to be criticizing:

> So far as we are taken up with the happenings in any novel in the same way in which we are taken up with what happens under our eyes, we are acquiring at least as much falsehood as truth. But when we are developed enough to say: "This is the view of life of a person who was a good observer within his limits, Dickens, or Thackeray, or George Elliot, or Balzac; but he looked at it in a different way from me . . . so what I am looking at is the world as seen by a particular mind"—then we are in a position to gain something from reading fiction. T. S. Eliot, "Religion and Literature," in *Essays Ancient and Modern*

Appendix

The Greek verb *mimeisthai* and such derivaties as *mimetikon* and *mimesis* can be translated, as normally employed up to Plato's time, as "imitate," "imitative," and "imitation" with as much accuracy as can be expected from any translation. Plato's extension of this use in book 3 of the *Republic* to denote the direct speech of the actor as opposed to narrative is natural enough, and any inaccuracy it might have as aesthetic theory can be excused in a disquisition on the principles of educational censorship. There is here no suggestion of fraud or misrepresentation but only of playing a part.

The extension in book 10 of the *Republic* is quite different, but equally natural. Here there is the notion of the imitation as a counterfeit, the notion as it occurs in "imitation pearl" or "imitation cream." Plato explains it with regard to a type of painting that was ultrarealistic and seriously aimed at *trompe-l'oeil* effects; there are anecdotes that show that this type of painting was well known in the fourth century B.C., when Plato was writing; Zeuxis is said to have painted grapes at which birds flew, and Apelles a horse at which live horses neighed. This style of painting could deceive children and fools at a distance, Plato tells us, more plausibly and moderately; it is the sort of painting that Plato is here calling mimetic, but it would be absurd to suppose that Plato thought it represented a serious threat to the well-being of society. The aspect of *mimesis* that Plato now goes on to ascribe to fiction no doubt includes its representational character; but the important aspect, as the story of the three beds shows, is its being a counterfeit of reality, a counterfeit of understanding, not of historical truth.

As the term *mimetic* was extended to cover the other arts, its connection with the root meaning of "imitation" was attenuated. To say that instrumental music is mimetic of the passions, as Aristotle does, can mean very little more than that such music can properly be called gay, sad. etc. Plato (*Laws* 669E) was unwilling to call purely instrumental music mimetic.

I do not believe that Plato thought that any other art would lay claims to insight as literature did, and so had no thought of banning any, though he wanted to purge them of undesirable elements. I dare say that such claims are sometimes made for painting nowadays, but they were not in Plato's time. If they had been he would no doubt have banished painting as well as mimetic poetry from the ideal state. The same fate would surely have befallen any art that made the same claims as poetry.

CHAPTER VI

What Could Go Wrong with Inspiration?
Why Plato's Poets Fail
Paul Woodruff

When poets are inspired, Plato tells us, they are out of their minds and possessed by gods; their role in making poetry is merely passive.[1] This account of inspiration is new with Plato,[2] but sits poorly with other Platonic statements about poetry and poets. If poetry is a gift of the gods, delivered through frenzied enthusiasts, how could there be anything wrong with it, either for poets or their audiences? Yet we know that Plato thought poetry could be very bad for audiences; and we should recognize that he finds poetry-making harmful to poets. Even when he treats poetry as among the greatest god-given goods (as he does in the *Phaedrus*), Plato judges poets harshly. That calls for an explanation. What could go wrong with inspiration, if it is communion with the divine?

(I ask this question specifically about the inspiration of mimetic poets because they, along with rhapsodes and orators, are in the worst condition, according to Plato. Other artists he might treat differently. I will not stop to ask why poetry and rhetoric are linked in this way; it has to do with the determination of both poetic and rhetorical language by formal, acoustic, and psychagogic considerations.)

We shall see that Plato thinks at least three things can go wrong with inspiration when it happens to poets: (1) inspired poetry-making is not motivated by love of the *kalon* ("the fine"); (2) it cannot issue in belief; and (3) it has no purpose of the sort that would define a *technē* ("skill"). Plato tells his new story about inspiration as possession partly because it implies these criticisms of poetry, and partly because the story itself is implied by claims made for inspired poetry (and so functions as an ironical *reductio ad absurdum*).

I shall argue that Plato is right in the way he characterizes poetry-making. The only defense for poets and poetry lovers is to disagree with Plato radically on the most basic issues: about the right motivation for human activities generally (including poetry), and about the nature of knowledge (which perhaps ought not to exclude inspiration).

The difference between inspiration and knowledge or understanding is the basis for Plato's sourness toward the arts, as Moravcsik observes. But Plato's attitude toward inspiration mixes sweet with sour. Poetry, he says, is one of the many good things in which gods are at work. And this should put poetry on a level with philosophy, for the presence of gods is felt also in the process that leads to understanding. So what is it that keeps poetic inspiration from being philosophy, or at least the beginning of philosophy? How could Plato's gods fail to bring about understanding in poets?

INSPIRATION AND TRUE BELIEF

Inspiration, *enthousiasmos,* is not a prerogative of poets, according to Plato. His conception of *enthousiasmos* as a good form of madness is derived from Bacchic Corybantic cults, in which a god is supposed to *possess* his *initiates* and drive them *out of their wits.* For what happens next—and anything can happen next—the initiate is not strictly responsible. The god acts through him. That is the important point for Plato and the Platonic Socrates: Inspiration negatives responsibility; you get no personal credit for the good you do while inspired. Socrates, to judge from the *Meno,* extended this conception of *enthousiasmos* to account for virtually any success in which teaching and learning play no part (99cd). Inspiration turns out to be amazingly widespread, for no one can give an account of what he does, let alone teach it to another, or show where he learned it.[3] Though the inspiration of poets is a traditional theme, a *palaios mythos* (*Laws* 719c), Socrates does not make a special case of poets. They are in the same boat with statesmen, and, we may infer, with all who fail Socrates' inhuman test. None deserves credit for the truths he says, uses, or believes; all are beneficiaries of a divine gift (*theia moira*).

Philosophers ought to be better off. But when he comes to talk of them, Plato treats philosophers too as recipients of divine favors. They look insane, but are actually inspired (*Phaedrus* 249d: *parakinein, enthousiazein*). They are initiates of the highest order, the only true initiates (*Phaedrus* 248c). They become as divine as is possible for a human being (*Republic* 6, 500cd, cf. *Sophist* 216ab). Their philosophical success, in a democracy at any rate, would be a divine gift (*Republic* 6, 493a).

Far from being the distinctive condition of poets or artists, inspiration turns out to be a common factor in Plato's explanations of human success. It is, at least in metaphor, what we have instead of the ideal education no one receives; it is what enables us to use true beliefs no one ever taught us. On this showing, Plato's complaint against poets ought to be the same as his complaint against all those whose beliefs are merely true, all whose beliefs do not amount to knowledge. The trouble with true belief is that you cannot teach it, were never taught it, and cannot defend it against Socrates. But no one, after all, can defend his beliefs against Socrates. And true belief, if you have it, will take you to Larissa as surely as knowledge will (*Meno* 97ab). The complaint is not severe. Why then is Plato particularly hard on poets? In the *Phaedrus,* where he cites poetry among the greatest goods, he ranks poets sixth on the nine levels of human degradation, barely above manual laborers, outranking besides them only tyrants and sophists. Poets are below philosophers,[4] of course, but also below kings, warriors, statesmen, businessmen, athletes, and prophets. Why does their inspiration do poets so little good? Their god-given truths should be as true as those of any athlete or businessman. But Plato must think there are varieties of inspiration, some worse than others, and the poets' inspiration worst of all. We do not know exactly why he thinks that. He leaves the details of inspiration, appropriately enough, a matter of mystery. But from various things he says about poets, we can reconstruct a Platonic account of what goes wrong for them.

MOTIVATION

Plato characteristically mentions inspiration as the source for things untutored people say. The experience of saying or believing things no one ever taught you is a common one, and particularly interesting to Plato. Mostly he calls it not *inspiration* but *recollection*. The best way to understand his view of poets is this: their inspiration is a case of recollection that has miscarried. It begins the right way, looking to things we call fine, and enjoying a productive sort of madness. But poetry goes the wrong way. Instead of seeking to ascend to the *kalon*, the ultimate source of its incipient recollection, poetry turns around and becomes enthralled with images of its own making. That is the first, and the most important, way in which poetry is self-contained (to use a key word from Moravcsik's chapter). Poets do not love the *kalon;* they love what they make.

Failure to love the *kalon* is common to all the lower eight levels of human degradation. It is not distinctive of poets. But it is a most surprising thing to say about poets, that they do not love the *kalon*, for *kalon* is often and most naturally translated "beauty," and poets, we think intuitively, are great lovers of beauty. For what other value would they work so hard? They do not do it for fame (most of them), or for money. Is Plato asking us to believe that they do not do it for beauty? How could he suggest, as he does in the *Phaedrus,* that a pederast stands a better chance than a poet of being *philokalos* ("fine-loving")?

Here we have a problem of translation. "Beautiful" translates *kalos* most precisely when it is used with reference to the way things appear to our senses, and less accurately when it is used in other ways.[5] I shall adopt Moravcsik's device of using "fine" for *kalos* as Plato generally uses it. I reserve "beautiful" for *kalos* when it is used for visible or audible beauty.

Plato's view, in a nutshell, is that beauty is not even a part of the fine, and that poets in loving beauty do not love the fine. He can grant our intuition; but he has an extraordinary conception of the *kalon*. In ordinary Greek usage, being beautiful (visibly *kalos*) is one very good way of being *kalos*. But Plato rejects that.

The basis of Plato's doctrine is his unitary conception of the fine, something he apparently took over from Socrates.[6] Socrates and Plato think there can be only one way of being fine, the same for everything that might be fine. To say that a person is fine in one way (in physical appearance, for example), but the opposite of fine in another way (morally, perhaps), is to commit a logical blunder.

Common usage allows that Alcibiades is fine because he is good-looking, but that his actions are not fine if they are immoral. On the other hand, Socrates will not let us draw the conclusion that Alcibiades is fine in body but not in soul. He wants us to determine which is the true way of being fine. That is the sort of choice he forces on his friends in Xenophon's *Symposium*. They, conforming to Greek usage, unanimously choose visible beauty.[7] But in other contexts, *kalos* was used of the real (invisible)value of a thing or action. So Socrates, true to his unitary conception of the fine, must insist on regarding mere beauty as a deception. A man, a horse, or a cooking spoon may be beautiful to look at, and still be utterly worthless. To call something fine when it is only beautiful is to court deception. This Socrates states in the *Hippias Major:* being *kalos* and being beautiful (that is, being visibly *kalos*) are two different things with different logical causes. What makes things *visibly* kalos is an *apatē peri to kalon* ("a deception about the fine"—293e–294e).

Socrates has good reasons for this. If there were more than one way of being fine, and the same thing could be fine (in one way) and not fine (in another way), then "fine" would turn out to be useless as a guide to human life. We could discover that Socrates is fine in his own way, and Alcibiades is fine in another. But then correctly calling someone "fine" would not help you decide whether to try becoming like him; for those two, Socrates and Alcibiades, would both be fine, and you might not be able to emulate both of them. Knowing what it is to be fine will be of no practical use to us if there are many different ways in which we could be fine. Socrates acts to safeguard the possibility that "fine" figure in an integrated account of the values that should guide human life. He assumes that there is one way of being fine, and declares that other ways are snares and delusions. Beauty is one of these. Fineness and goodness must be firmly identified (cf. *Hippias Major* 297c).

Plato, with his more complex metaphysics, dismisses mere beauty more subtly. Beautiful objects or qualities are only images *(eikones)* of the fine, and the true lover sees them for what they are *(Phaedrus* 250b4). The *Republic* tells us what is wrong with them: the many beautiful things, the beauties of sight and hearing, are not purely *(eilikrinōs)* fine. They are rolled around in the twilight world of belief between *being* fine and *not being* fine; they no more are, than are not, fine (479ab). It should follow that lovers of these beauties, the lovers of sights and sounds, are not lovers of the fine. Plato effectively draws that conclusion in the *Phaedrus* when he makes of the *philokaloi* a small philosophical elite (248d).

Defenders of poetry have two choices. If they think poetry is motivated by love of beauty, they should attack Plato's integrated system of values. It is not that Plato has no special place for beauty; he has no place for it whatever. It is an image, a deception, a fake. We might want to rehabilitate beauty, and set it up as a rival to fineness-goodness, if we are prepared to divide our loyalties between two different sorts of values and to give up hope of "an integrated account of the well-lived human life" (as Moravcsik puts it). The unlikely alternative, of course, is to unseat fineness-goodness altogether, and put beauty in its place.

But now that we find Plato willing to grant poets a love of beauty, we may want to change our minds. Are poets merely lovers of sights and sounds? True, sights and sounds are precisely what a dramatic poet has to offer us. But mere beauty hardly seems the aim of tragedy, ancient or modern. We might hope to find a motivation for poetry toward which Plato would be kinder. But here we meet an obstacle. Plato is surely right that poets do not and cannot love the Platonic form of the fine. They would be Platonic philosophers if they did, and their love would find expression not in poetry but in life itself—the life of a philosopher, ideally, statecraft.

KNOWLEDGE: THE PROBLEM OF BELIEF

So far we have said nothing to explain why Plato ranks poets beneath athletes and businessmen. None but the elite knowingly loves the *kalon;* so in this respect poets are no worse than the rest of us. Why, then, does their inspiration not win them a higher position?

The answer is simply that the inspiration of poets is so powerful it leaves them no role in poetry-making, and consequently no credit for their poems. The good qualities of a poem cannot rub off on its author, for the most beautiful poem can sing through the mouth of the worst of poets (*Ion* 534e6). Making poems is not evidence of any sort of knowledge or ability. Poets cannot know *that* their poems are true, because, as we shall see, they cannot even believe them. And they cannot know *how* to make their poems, because poems lack the sort of function that would define a case of knowing *how*.

Let us begin with the problem of belief. If poems were true (as gifts of the gods they ought to be true), and if poets believed them, then poets would acquire true beliefs by inspiration, and should rank with statesmen. But poets rank far below statesmen and other true believers; so it is a reasonable inference that Plato thinks poets do not believe the truths they utter. An inspired prophet like the Pythia is barred from understanding what she says by the very madness that allows her to speak prophecy (*Timaeus* 71e); and we might suppose that the same goes for poets. But poets, unlike prophets, do not speak in tongues, so the cases are not analogous. If Plato wants us to agree that poets do not believe what they say, he will have to give us a better reason than that they are too crazed with inspiration to understand their own poems.

This better reason is easily given for dramatic poets, and may be extended with some difficulty to epic and lyric writers. What inspiration gives a playwright is a thousand or so lines of dialogue in verse, divided into speeches that are appropriate for different mythical characters in different mythical situations. No one person could believe all of those speeches. But if a playwright cannot believe what she says as a playwright, she cannot take the first step in understanding, for that would be dialectic, which depends absolutely on the Socratic rule that those who practice it try always to say what they believe. But a playwright says only what other people would believe at some other time in some other place.[8]

Nevertheless, a play may *contain* or *express* believable truths, even though the work taken as a whole is unbelievable. Certain lines contained in a play might be god's truth, and their author might be lucky enough to believe them. But (1) to consider a line in her play as a candidate for belief, she must abstract it from its dramatic context. So considered, the line is no longer dramatic, and so not a counterexample to the principle that dramatic poetry is beyond belief. And (2) our playwright may be the equal of

Euripides or Sophocles, and still have no firm opinion as to which of the lines she has given her characters are true.[9] We may conclude that whatever gift a playwright has stops short of teaching her what to think about the problems she depicts.

But what of truths that may not be uttered in a play, but are expressed in some manner by the entire work? For tragedy they would be "pride goes before a fall," for example, or "human life is miserable." These too, taken by themselves, are not dramatic or poetic. More important, we do not need to be told such clichés, and certainly not by the gods. If dramatic inspiration yields knowledge, it should produce something more exciting and definitely more dramatic.

What a dramatic poet gets by inspiration is a *drama*, and that is not the sort of thing she can believe. Such inspiration, therefore, cannot issue in belief; *a fortiori* it could not deliver knowledge, if knowledge requires belief.

Similar arguments could be developed for lyric and epic poetry, but at much greater length.[10] Plato is concerned chiefly with dramatic poetry, and for that the case is clear.

This feature of poetic inspiration—that it is beyond belief—is unique. The inspiration of prophets can lead eventually to belief. When she comes to understand what she has said, on returning to her senses, even the Pythia (the prophetess at Delphi) could on principle understand her divine message. So here is another defect of poetic inspiration, and one that sets poetry apart from other degrading activities. Even when a poet says the truth, she does not believe it (at least, not *qua* poet). And this is another way in which poetry is self-contained: it is insulated from the belief structure of its author.

KNOWLEDGE: THE PROBLEM OF SKILL

The third defect of poetic inspiration is this: it leaves no scope for a *technē* ("skill") of poetry. When you let the god take over your mind, you give up the chance to become *technikos*. Everything you seem to do is done through you by the god.[11] Rhapsodes and rhetoricians are no better off in this respect than poets.[12] But others we call artists fare differently.[13]

That there is no *technē* of poetry is an obvious consequence of

Plato's radical account of inspiration as possession. But he has good independent grounds for asserting this. A *technē* subordinates an activity to what after Aristotle we would call a final cause. A man with a *technē* can explain and justify what he does in his profession on the grounds that it is necessary for some distinct and valuable end. Plato rightly insists that poets cannot do that. What, after all, could be the final cause of a tragic play? Aristotle suggests it is *catharsis,* but he seems unable to show how all the necessary parts of a tragedy are necessary for *that.* And far from agreeing with him that *catharsis* is what tragedies are for, we do not even agree with each other about what Aristotle intended by the word. In fact, a tragic play draws our attention and pleases us by generating a medley of emotions, and entertaining us besides, but also by presenting itself as something to be valued for its own sake. That is part of what is meant by "the autonomy of art." Since tragic poetry is self-contained in this way, we cannot expect a tragic playwright to justify what he does with reference to a single final cause, a distinct, separable thing that it is for. The best she could do would be to point to the entire play as the end, and insist that everything she put in the play was necessary for *that.* But a workman could explain any product in that way, however incomplete or badly botched it might be. All the parts are necessary for any whole. By contrast, the parts that are necessary for a bridle are necessary for the bridle to serve its function, and a bridlemaker can explain what he does with reference to the use of bridles. The trouble with poetry-making is that such an explanation is not available to the poet. He does not really know why his poems are the way they are. It is not that poems have no use; they can have a bewildering variety of uses. The problem is that identifying its possible uses does not explain why a poem is what it is.[14]

To this we are likely to object. We might suppose, carelessly, I think, that poets have some *technai*—skills at prosody or diction, for example—that they apply to the pleasing expression of what they were inspired to say. But Plato disagrees. He will not allow the poets a *technē,* even of pure style.[15] All the beauty of a poem comes from the inspiring gods. Plato does not distinguish stylistic skill from the other gifts poets have.

Here we must agree with him. It would be ludicrous to

distinguish style from message in poetry in such a way as to assign responsibility for style to poets, and for message to gods. The stylistic features of a poem are usually much more godlike than the message, which, if it can be abstracted from the poem at all, is bound to be prosaic, and more than likely banal.

Poetry has no distinct explanatory function; consequently, poets have no skills. They do not have knowledge *how* to do anything, because there is nothing we can put our fingers on that they know how to do. The self-containment of poetry means that poets have neither knowledge *that* their products are true, nor knowledge *how* to produce them.

INSPIRATION AS POSSESSION

At this point I owe it to the poets to examine Plato's account of inspiration more critically. Plato thinks poets are not at all responsible for the good that might crop up in their poems. They are mere passive mouthpieces for the gods. Now, Plato must have noticed that this is ridiculous.[16] If it were true, poets would speak with the same unanimity Plato attributes to the gods. Poets should agree about everything. And because gods do not disguise themselves, poets would speak clearly, without mystification. But poets do not agree with each other. A dramatic poet *has* to utter contradictory speeches. And all poets, it seems, speak in riddles and disguise their meaning. No god could be responsible for such a mess (on Plato's assumptions). Why should gods speak to us at all, if they intend such a bouillabaisse of riddles and contradictions? Better that they keep silent. Plato's story about gods and passive poets is absurd, and he cannot be sincere when he tells it.[17]

But if the story is false, and goes far beyond anything poets would claim on their own account, why does Plato tell it with such alarming consistency? It cannot be that he is following a tradition, because Plato, here as on so many subjects, is an innovator (see n. 2 above). He speaks with irony, of course, and obviously with animosity against poets. But why this particular falsehood?

To that question I have two compelling answers. The first is that Plato has rightly caught the poets and their supporters in a paradox. They want to claim some authority for their work, on the grounds that it is inspired. (They apparently do not think they can claim it on any other grounds.) We are prepared with Plato to grant authority to the utterances of experts. But poets are not, and do not claim to be, experts on anything but poetry-making. That is why they appealed to divine sources in the first place. If poetry were authoritative, then, it would be so because its mysterious source would be an expert. The poets who gave it voice would have no personal authority in the matter. They must vacate their bodies, so to speak, and let the god speak through them, if their words are to carry the authority of the god. They must be utterly possessed. And that absurd account of poetry-making is merely a consequence of the claim that poetry is authoritative because inspired. Plato's false account of poetic experience is a *reductio ad absurdum* of claims made for poets.

The second reason why Plato tells his story about inspiration is that, for all its irony, it has true consequences. If poets were overwhelmingly inspired, there would, as Plato says, be no credit for knowledge to them in their poetry. Even if their poetry were true, they would not believe it; even if it were well made, they would not have known how to make it.

Plato's radical account of inspiration implies that poets do not exhibit those sorts of knowledge in making poetry. And that consequence, I have argued, is true. However you explain it, poetry-making cannot produce the kind of thing that can be believed or known the way beliefs may be known. And whatever gifts poets have, they lack a poetic *technē;* there is no end they know how to achieve that would explain every important feature of their poetry. There is nothing in poetry-making to define the sort of how-to knowledge that craftsmen have. Poetry is too much self-contained to exhibit knowledge *how* or knowledge *that.*

If we want to defend the poets, we should start by admitting that Plato is right that poetry-making will not support poetic claims to those sorts of knowledge. After that, two courses are open to us. We might argue on the one hand for the values of things Plato ignores—taste and sensitivity, for example, things that *are* displayed in poetry-making. On the other hand, we could stay with Plato's integrated scheme of values, over which knowledge presides with a luster irresistible to philosophers. If we do that, we will have to quarrel with the limited conception of knowledge I have so far attributed to Plato. Some poets are better than others; and the better ones appear to be wiser in respect of some sort of knowledge. If that intuition is right, there ought to be another sort of knowledge, knowledge that is not a matter of things to believe or things to accomplish, and this could be the knowledge of poets. What it is, and why Plato should be urged to make space for it, are questions for another, more epistemological, occasion.

NOTES

1. I am indebted to Julius Moravcsik, whose chapter "Noetic Aspiration and Artistic Inspiration" got me well started on this line of thought; and I owe thanks for asking good questions to Alexander Nehamas, Richard Patterson, and Robert Solomon.

This chapter is one of the fruits of a junior fellowship at the Center for Hellenic Studies. I received additional support from the Research Institute of the University of Texas. I hereby express my gratitude to both institutions.

The best and most complete account of the subject is E. N. Tigerstedt, *Plato's Idea of Poetical Inspiration, Commentationes Humanarum Litterarum,* vol. 44, no. 2 (Helsinki: Societas Scientiarum Fennica-1969). Tigerstedt offers a sober interpretation of each relevant text, together with a useful review of the more important scholarly opinions.

2. Cicero says Democritus had the same idea (*DK* 68B17); if he is right, Democritus would probably have given the idea to Plato. But ancient authorities seem to have confused Plato and Democritus on this point, and there is no hard evidence that Democritus conceived of inspiration as *possession.* Tigerstedt argues persuasively for Plato's originality in this matter (op. cit., p. 64ff; cf. his "Furor Poeticus," *Journal of the History of Ideas,* XXXI [1970], 163–78).

3. Inspiration is attributed to poets and rhapsodes in the *Ion,* to poets at *Apology* 22cd and *Meno* 99cd, to statesmen at *Meno* 99d, and to bad philosophers at *Theaetetus* 180b4 and *Philebus* 15e1. Socrates ironically claims inspiration for himself in the *Cratylus* 396d2, 7 and frequently in the *Phaedrus* (for example, 235c6 and 263d2). Cf. *Crito* 54d.

4. The first class is described as "of the man . . . who is wisdom-loving *(philosophos)* or fine-loving *(philokalos)* or cultivated and a lover *(mousikos kai erōtikos).*" Such a man, we may assume, is a philosopher and a lover of the fine if he meets with the proper education, but otherwise merely a cultivated lover (one in whom proper education has led to self-restraint). There is no support for the tempting mistranslations "artist" or "follower of the Muses" (Jowett and Hackforth, respectively).

5. The English word "beautiful" actually has most of the range of *kalos;* but unlike *kalos* its most basic uses are in regard to sights and sounds. Moreover,

"beautiful" and the modern European words it translates have a special history in art criticism and a special association with the art world. To call something "beautiful" is to bring it into the shadow of the world of art. But *kalos* has no such associations.

6. Though radical, Socrates' position was developed out of a traditional strain in Greek thought. That is why his opponents (Xenophon's symposiasts, the lovers of sights and sounds in the *Republic*, Hippias in the *Hippias Major*) have nothing to say against him on this point. See W. H. A. Adkins, *Merit and Responsibility: A Study in Greek Values* (Oxford University Press, 1960), p. 163.

7. Xenophon, *Symposium V. Kalos* was used of persons at this time with reference to their appearance. See K. J. Dover, *Greek Popular Morality in the Time of Plato and Aristotle* (Berkeley: University of California Press, 1974), p. 69.

8. Plato makes the basic point at *Laws* 719c. Unlike a lawgiver, a dramatic poet speaks on both sides of the issues he treats, without knowing which side is right.

A philosopher writing like Plato in dialogues would appear to be vulnerable to the same criticism, for such a philosopher speaks on both sides of many issues, and whatever gift he has for writing dialogue does not tell him which side to believe. But there is an important difference between playwrights and philosophers. If a playwright knows anything *qua* playwright, he must display it in his plays. Nothing else could be evidence for playwrightly knowledge. But a philosopher's gift (Plato believes) must be *hidden* in his writing. His knowledge is already established by the life he leads, particularly by live dialectic. His dialogue is supposed at best to remind readers of things both know independently, and in the proper sense philosophically. Plays are not reminders in the same way. (See Moravcsik, p. 42.)

9. Scholars cannot agree on where the authors of *Antigone* and the *Bacchae* stood on the issues of those plays; but no responsible critic blames the poets (as poets) for not telling us what they think.

10. I want to contrast the attitude of a poet toward his poem against that of a researcher, say, toward his results. A researcher seeks results he can believe; but a poet wants to make a poem toward which he takes a different attitude. This is partly owing to the importance in poetry of acoustic devices (rhyme and meter), and also to the frequency in poetry of metaphor and other peculiar uses of words that (I would argue) defy literal belief. Once we are clear about the poet's attitude toward his poem, we can begin to consider properly such questions as whether there is poetical truth.

11. Socrates insists that no *sophia* is displayed by poets (*Apology* 22cd, *Meno* 99cd). This is probably tantamount to the *Ion's* implication that poets have no *technē* (533e). I would take *sophia* here as a synonym for *technē* in the special sense (but see Tigerstedt, *Plato's Idea of Poetical Inspiration*, p. 53). The *Phaedrus* says merely that *technē* is not sufficient to make a poet (245a), but that is consistent with the idea that poets have no skills.

The *Laws* speaks of poets' mimetic skill (719c), and this rather minor skill may be allowed to poets. It is, merely, the skill that achieves verisimilitude.

In the end of the *Symposium* Socrates entertains the possibility of a dramatic *technē*; but since it would make the same man a tragic and a comic poet, this is clearly a *technē* no one has (*Symposium* 223d).

12. The *Ion* makes this claim about rhapsodes. Socrates claims inspiration for himself as an orator (with heavy irony) in the *Phaedrus* (235c, 263d), and there it is important that he credits the inspiring deities with whatever stylistic virtues his false speech possesses.

Elsewhere Socrates denies that rhetoric is a *technē* on similar grounds (it is *alogon pragma*), but without mentioning inspiration. Although he entertains the idea that a good and skillful rhetoric could be developed (in the *Phaedrus*), he holds out no such hopes for poetry.

13. See Terence Irwin, *Plato's Moral Theory: The Early and Middle Dialogues* (Oxford University Press, 1977), p. 74. Music and sculpture were firmly esconced as *technai*, and Plato apparently had no objection to that.

14. Edgar Allan Poe vigorously contests the point. Writing of his own procedure in making *The Raven,* he insists that poems are properly developed out of a consideration for the *effects* they are to produce. I am quite convinced that many good authors do proceed in that way. But the effects of various poems (the sorts of effects Poe has in mind, chiefly "a pleasurable elevation of the soul") are so much the same that talk of effects cannot explain the striking variety of poetry. Nonfunctional variations in bridles are incidental to their being bridles, and call for no explanation; but variety in poetry appears to be essential to it. E. A. Poe, "The Philosophy of Composition," *Graham's Magazine of Literature and Art,* 28 (1846), 163–64; excerpted in Albert Rothenberg and Carl R. Hausman, *The Creativity Question* (Durham, N.C.: 1976), pp. 57–61.

15. This is the implication of *Ion* 534e6, and also of the discussion at *Phaedrus* 263d, where Socrates credits the gods with the organization of his speech.

16. Even the most ecstatic of modern poets is unable to hold that view of inspiration consistently. Rimbaud writes of himself as the brass "that wakes up to find itself a trumpet," and with one image after another emphasizes the utter passivity of the poetic process. But he concludes, ". . . the poet is truly a thief of fire!" (Letter to Paul Demeny [May 15, 1871], trans. Louise Varèse in *Illuminations* (New York: New Directions, 1957), pp. xxix–xxxi; cf. p. xxvii.

17. A number of scholars disagree. (See Tigerstedt, *Plato's Idea of Poetical Inspiration,* p. 50) But as Tigerstedt observes, no plainly nonironical passage tells the radical inspiration story. The famous second speech of the *Phaedrus* is framed in irony, and contains serious criticism of the poets as well. See *Phaedrus* 265bc for Socrates' own evaluation of the speech; and note that for all its overblown poetical language, Socrates does not call it inspired. It is, instead, a product of his own ability (*dunamis*—257a3), with poetical language added to please Phaedrus. Socrates claims inspiration only for the first speech he gave, which, he later insists, was false. So Plato never has Socrates speak sincerely of poetic inspiration, and this no doubt means that Plato knew that what Socrates had to say about inspiration was not strictly true.

Tigerstedt finds Plato's most serious words on the subject in the *Timaeus* (71e–72b), where he discusses inspired prophecy (Tigerstedt, pp. 71–72). There he says that an inspired prophet is out of his mind, and therefore cannot understand what he says; inspired utterances must be interpreted by sane (uninspired) and reasonable people. This could be Plato's final view on poetry as well—that poetry has a divine source but needs to be interpreted by philosophers. It is an attractive idea to attribute to Plato, but has no clear textual warrant. And the analogy between poetry and prophecy breaks down. Prophets speak in "tongues" only a specialist can decipher; but any Greek can make a go of interpreting Homer.